02806

Fellowship for Today
Lending Library

You are preparing a permanent record for our library,
so please print or write legibly.

Title: __Friends in High Places__

Author: __Thomas Shepherd__

☒ book   ☐ audio cassette   ☐ videotape

☐ other (please specify): _____

This item is a: ☒ gift   ☐ loan

UN

Given by: _____

on ___/___/_____   (name)

FRIENDS IN HIGH PLACES

by
Thomas Shepherd

Unity Books
Unity Village, Missouri 64065

Cover design by Sue Jackson

LLC: 85-052214
ISBN: 0-87159-040-9

Dedication

For my mother, who gave me life, and my grandmother, who gave me language.

Unity is a link in the great educational movement inaugurated by Jesus Christ. Our objective is to discern the Truth and prove it. The Truth we teach is not new, neither do we claim special discovery of new religious principles. Our purpose is to help and teach mankind to use and prove the eternal Truth taught by the Master.—*Charles Fillmore*

Contents

Introduction

Afterword

Introduction

A Short Course in Epistemology

A lot has happened since Jesus walked among us. Wars and rumors of wars, periods of peace and cultural advancement, outpourings of creative genius, and terrible repressions against the human spirit. Christianity began in a humble manger and grew to mighty thrones. Christian theology, which is organized reflection on the Divine from a Christocentric perspective, has achieved great insights and succumbed other times to great temptations. We who study Truth principles struggle to affirm the good in our lives and affairs. Yet the whole history of Christianity has not been pleasant. There are ghosts in the basement, clanking about in their great iron chains and threatening to creep up the back stairs some dark night and catch us unaware.

Much harm has been done in the name of God and in misbegotten service to the Prince of Peace. Anyone who studies Christian history must begin with a frank admission: we have not always loved our neighbor as we love ourselves. Any study of the Christian faith that does not face the ghosts in the basement will be unable to point to the angels on our balconies.

In this work we shall look at some of those ghosts and angels, with an appropriate emphasis on the "good guys." There are heroes who fought lonely battles, original thinkers who nudged human consciousness along its painfully slow but unmistakable upward path. All too often Truth students reject the whole heritage of Christian theology because all they have heard are the ghosts rambling in the inner depths of the house of faith. If the idea of Christian theology conjures up only the ghosts—stern authoritarians who demand that you believe all manner of nonsense—you will hear a different refrain in the pages of this study.

There is another tune in the great symphony of Christian theology. A melody humming in the background much of the time, now and again it takes center stage as the whole orchestra of the faith seizes its delicious tune and plays it grandly for a season. Then discordant music arises and the sweet, persistent melody falls into oblivion once more, returning to a mere humming of the ancient music. We did not create the tune; we inherited it from our ancestors in the faith. Most Truth students are unaware of how indebted we are to those heroes and heroines of the past, our great forefathers and foremothers of the Christian Church.

Truth students are fond of using the word *metaphysical* to describe their studies and spiritual exercises. There is another word that may better describe what we are trying to accomplish, a term which has a long and distinguished history in Christian thought. The word is *mysticism*. Those who practice this way of religion are called *mystics*.

Every faith has produced mystics. Every religious hierarchy has viewed the mystic with mistrust. The mystic has usually responded by pronouncing those hierarchies as betrayers of the faith; the hierarchy has usually replied by excommunicating the heretical mystic. There is something about mysticism, that raises the hairs on the back of the neck of religious authority.

The mystic wants no go-between standing in the holy place for him, distributing to him the divine graces. Mystics share one passion: to know God personally. To experience God, to feel God's presence and not just read about God in a book—these are the goals of mysticism.

His or her rewards for pursuing the mystical path are increased consciousness and direct inspiration from the Divine. Rather than the sublime God-concept of the philosophers, the mystic wants a God who walks with him and talks with him. He seeks not the God of Descartes, Spinoza, and Whitehead, but the God of Moses, David, and Jesus.

In all fairness to the religious hierarchies, we need to acknowledge that they do have a point. How does one know when something gleaned in mystical communion is an authentic insight from God? Recognizing our own guidance is sometimes difficult. How shall we respond to those among us who claim to have special revelations from the Divine? Shall we take seriously every person who stands and shouts, "Thus saith the Lord"? I knew a minister who said that religion is a way for some people to be socially acceptably crazy and get away with it. If you think you're Napoleon, you're considered a mental case. If you think you're the prophet Elijah, you're considered a religious person.

If the mystic is correct when he affirms that Truth comes directly from God—as he must be—how does a person measure contradictory truths? One cannot survey the current religious landscape without discovering many religious philosophies, all claiming some sort of direct guidance and yet disagreeing vehemently with one another. It is not a new problem.

An ancient Jewish parable tells of a heated debate among rabbis over some point in the law. After much discussion, one of the contenders leaped up and proclaimed that he knew his viewpoint was correct because an angel from heaven appeared to him and revealed it. How could an angel be wrong? After a moment of quiet reflection, another rabbi replied that the Torah was given to men, not angels. They would have to decide what was true for themselves.

Lessons from Luther

It is the same problem in every age. Let's take a historic example. When Martin Luther began the Protestant Reformation, he had no idea he was opening a door to a new religious world. He was just pursuing his own quest for Truth as a scholar and an ultra-pious monk. Luther was troubled with practices in the church of his day, which he considered to be excessive and un-Christian, so he wrote a list of "Ninety-Five Theses" for debate and discussion in the academic/theological community and posted it on the bulletin board at the University of Wittenberg. The "bulletin board" at the University was the great wooden door of the Castle Church. The date was October 31, 1517.

Written in Latin and intended exclusively for academia, the "Ninety-Five Theses" were soon translated into German and other modern languages. Luther's list became a topic of rage and rejoicing in the capitals of sixteenth-century Europe. Obscure Dr. Luther found himself *de facto* leader of a new movement that was breaking out of centuries of wandering in arid absurdity and foraging into greener pastures of the spirit.

As the acclaimed leader of a new school of thought, Luther faced some stiff opposition. He was challenging papal authority, church councils, creeds and practices stretching back through the high Middle Ages to the edge of apostolic times.

Yet his greatest opposition might have come from within himself. Martin Luther had doubted his adequacy from the earliest days of his childhood. Raised by stern parents who whipped the fear of God into him, the mature Luther sought to earn God's approval through whipping himself by excesses in fasting, self-denial, and fervent prayer. He became an Augustinian monk, and by his own admission he was a fanatic.

Finally Luther discovered another way. Through reading the Scripture, Luther learned the New Testament/Pauline doctrine of *salvation by faith*. We would say the gate house to spiritual growth is consciousness, not through mystical practices, meditation, or good works alone. These are fine exercises, but the only way to Christ consciousness is through affirming that we are one with God. Luther was not prepared to go all the way and teach the divinity of humanity, of course. A child of his own era, he still harbored mistrust for human character and professed a belief in a power of evil. But he opened the door for others when he insisted that individual conscience, guided by the Holy Spirit, must be the basis for interpreting one's faith. He based his theology on the Bible, which he said must be read by individual believers and interpreted by them. Not the authority of council or creed, but the authority of Holy Scripture, individually interpreted, would be the polar star of Lutheranism.

Almost immediately his opponents pointed to a problem in any theology based on individual interpretation. *"Bist du alein klug?"* (Are you alone right?) they taunted him. Who are you, a mere man, to stand against all that the Church has taught for centuries? Everyone has always believed as we believe, so who do you think you are, coming along and upsetting so many centuries of true teaching with your heretical babbling?

A lesser man would have sunk into despair never to rise again. But Martin Luther was a great hero of the faith who knew Church history as well as Holy Scripture. Abandon the field to the forces of orthodoxy? Not a chance! He could cite countless theologians who stood with him on the great issues. A heresy? No way! His teaching was just a modern renewal of the ancient faith taught by Jesus and the apostles.

Luther knew that Christianity is less a coherent system of belief than a family of sub-religions, more a marketplace than an assembly line. Like any other institution, the Christian Church has always had its schools of thought. Some teachers saw the Christ event one way, another group saw it differently. Although the phenomenon of denominationalism is relatively new, there have always been groups and subgroups within Christendom. Luther knew he could call upon a large number of witnesses to testify in behalf of the case he was trying to make, great thinkers and teachers who saw that faith rather than works in the outer world was the key to salvation.

The issues of Luther's day no longer incite riots among us as they did in sixteenth-century Europe. But the same question continues to plague religious thinkers down to our times: *Bist du alein klug?* Are you alone right? What makes you think your religious viewpoint is correct when there are so many sincere, intelligent people who see the faith in a radically different manner?

The question, "How can we decide what is true?" is known to theology and philosophy as *epistemology*. It is the first question any theologian must answer, albeit unconsciously, before sitting down to write his magnum opus.

In the centuries before our own, religious thinkers liked to codify their convictions by composing creeds and confessions. The theory was that if we can boil down all the theological verbiage into a clear essence, such as a perfect statement of faith in a creed, we could then insist that everyone abide by the words of the creed and insure everyone would get to heaven. In the past, some felt justified in torturing people to death in order to force them to agree to the statement, because if their immortal souls were at stake, why, what's a few hours of agony when compared to eternal bliss?

The poverty of this line of thought is obvious from our vantage point in this scientific age. Humanity has a miserable track record at attaining perfect statements of faith but a long history of inflicting torture upon men and women anyway.

Creeds and confessions fail to take into account the evolutionary nature of human consciousness. We change and grow while creeds remain static. Accordingly, modern Christian theology has generally adopted a dynamic/dialectical methodology. Instead of perfect statements that will be true forever, the departure point for most modern theologies is an epistemology based on guiding principles that interact with each other dialectically. Not a voice from Mount Olympus, but a workshop. Not one way alone to interpret the ancient faith, but a series of important factors to consider involving theology today or at any time in the future.

The Model for Modern Mystics

One large protestant body, the United Methodist Church, has suggested a system of dialectical theology based on four poles of reference. Instead of standing on any one authority source, this dynamic approach to epistemology says that there are at least four reference points for Christians. This model suggests that when considering a religious question, we bring the idea into dialogue with these four great sources of theological reflection: Scripture, tradition, experience, reason (see figure 1).

The reference points interact so that no single source, such as the Bible, is allowed to overwhelm the others. In fact, a person is free to let these four be in conflict with each other, as they often are in reality, without feeling disloyal to the Christian faith. Are there ideas in the Bible which seem repulsive to reason and life experience? Are there things happening in the world today against which the biblical witness cries out? Does your power of reason tell you that a traditional idea just will not work for you? Are you comfortable with a church tradition and want to give yourself permission to enjoy it because it has deeper insights into Truth?

This model allows a mix-and-match theology. It is not a license to be irresponsible, because a balanced theology will employ all four in dialogue with each other. Martin Luther emphasized the Bible so much that the great cry of the Reformation became, "Sola Scriptura!" (Only the Scripture). On closer examination, however, we can see that Luther used reason, experience, and the ideas

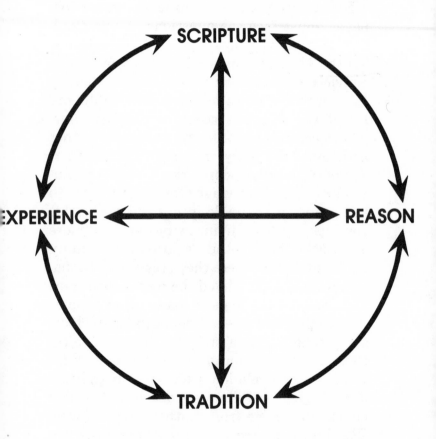

Figure 1

of other theologians (tradition) while constructing his theological framework.

Every religious organization, every believer, must face the questions of epistemology. How do we know that what we believe is Truth? The problem is complicated by a deep conviction that every person can, as Charles Fillmore did, "go to headquarters." Fillmore found the religious scene of the late nineteenth century as confusing as Martin Luther had found the early sixteenth. Like Luther, Fillmore decided people don't need institutions to tell them what God wants them to know since we have Scripture and can read it correctly through divine inspiration. Fillmore and Luther both withdrew into private study and meditation where they received illumination by which they lived the rest of their lives and changed the lives of many other people.

Both pioneers opened doors to let fresh air and sunlight into a stagnant house of faith. Both faced the charge of heresy and of inventing a new religion, which they both hotly denied. Here is Fillmore's declaration which could have come from Luther's pen as well: *The Truth we teach is not new, neither do we claim special discovery of new religious principles. Our purpose is to help and teach mankind to use and prove the eternal Truth taught by the Master.*

It has been my observation in visiting with and serving as a guest speaker at various Truth churches that modern mystical/metaphysical Christianity does a great job with three of the four elements of the four-point model suggested. We have made great strides toward a modern understanding of the historical-analytical method of biblical interpretation and are pairing those insights with the metaphysical interpretations gleaned from studying the cryptic symbolism of Hebrew and Greek words. We never shirk from learning from experience, and we readily engage our powers of reason in both intuitive/right-brain and intellectual/left-brain thinking.

But bring us up to bat against that old devil tradition and we often strike out. Unity students are usually emigrants from other spiritual lands. We tend to be a refugee church. Sometimes, therefore, we have a tendency to stigmatize the traditional church because it didn't have what we wanted. So the word *tradition* leaves a bad taste in many a Truth student's mouth.

That, of course, is a complete misunderstanding of what the traditional church really is. There is no need to cast our whole Christian heritage overboard because we've had some theological problems.

We do metaphysical interpretation in which we find root meanings of biblical words and then search for deeper insights through allegory. That method was created by Philo Judaeus in the first century A.D.

We teach that all people will be saved eventually, that there is no hell, and that all people are basically good. Origen said this in the second century, and Pelagius said it in the fifth.

God and man are one? Hardly a new idea. Christ consciousness the goal? Old stuff, my friends, available in the writings of medieval churchmen like John Scotus Erigena and Meister Eckehart.

In fact, you would be hard pressed to name a single spiritual teaching held by Unity today that has not been proclaimed by Christian theologians of an earlier era. We stand as heirs to a long heritage of mystical theology as ancient and traditional as any other element in the many schools of Christian thought. Too long have Truth students allowed the hyper-orthodox and fundamentalist fringe to crowd them off the field of Christian history. Too readily have we abandoned our rightful place as a legitimate school of thought in the diverse household of Christianity. Our belief system is as old as the Bible, and our insights are as "traditional" as those of our other brothers and sisters in the faith.

We represent mystical Christianity. It is time we claimed that heritage as our own, as it surely is.

But how do we find that mystical heritage? How can we bring to bear the great insights of mystical/metaphysical Christianity when we are working on our theology? If there is a long history of teachers and thinkers who have shared our inclinations toward a theology of God's goodness, wouldn't it be nice to know who they are? Wouldn't it be a joy to learn that we are, in our own way, just as orthodox as our highly liturgical fellows down the street? Furthermore, wouldn't it be delightful to learn that some of the teachings Unity has been proclaiming for nearly a century are *just now* coming up on the agenda for serious discussion in modern theology?

Wouldn't it be amazing to discover that the time for mystical/metaphysical Christianity has not yet fully arrived, that the little melody humming in the wings is gaining strength once more, and that we may be singing the opening bars to a whole symphony of ideas which will harmonize the Christian faith in the twenty-first century and beyond?

If you find this scenario appealing, you are cordially invited to read on and be amazed, surprised, and delighted. Believe it or not, you are about to meet a whole pack of strangers who will sound very familiar to you. They are your long-lost relatives in the ancient faith. They are the angels on the balconies of Christendom. They are your Friends in High Places.

Part I

Jewish Roots and Christian Branches

1

Father of
Metaphysical Interpretation
Philo Judaeus
(1st Century A.D.)

He paused, pen in hand, pondering the problem. Beneath the window of his study, merchants hawked trade goods from the farthest corners of the Roman Empire. Spicy smells of noonday cooking rose from the twisted streets and alleys of the great city around him. Built three hundred years earlier by Alexander the Great, first-century Alexandria stood second only to Rome as a commercial and population center. As an intellectual center, it stood second to none.

The library at Alexandria would be remembered as the first place where organized research into the nature of life and the world was conducted. The library housed the finest collection of ancient manuscripts the world has ever known. But Alexandria was even more than this. It was religious shrines, temples, and schools. Theological ideas from across the wide, pluralistic Greco-Roman world were celebrated and debated there. Hellenism, that elegant cosmopolitan mixture of classical Greek thought and Roman practicality, found its highest expression in Alexandria. Oriental mystery cults rubbed shoulders with sophisticated schools of Greek philosophy in an atmosphere of free exchange and exciting new ideas.

Yet, this ancient metropolis provided fertile ground for more than just a host of pagan cults and philosophies; Judaism thrived there, too. Ancient writers claimed the Jewish population numbered one million in Egypt, and most of them lived in Alexandria. Although modern scholars such as Samuel Sandmel question this astronomical figure, they generally agree that there was an enormous number of Jews at Alexandria.[1] In the days of Jesus, Jews represented one-tenth of the population of the Roman Empire, perhaps as many as eight million. Most of them lived away from the Holy Land in Alexandria, Babylon, and even Rome.

It was one of these Children of Israel who paused that day to reflect on the relationship between his two worlds. His name is Philo, but he would come to be known as Philo Judaeus or Philo of Alexandria. He was the son of a wealthy Jewish family. Weaned on the Torah and Greek classics, he learned to love both; yet the two seemed to most persons irreconcilable. What connection could there be between the world of Homer, Plato, and Aristotle and that of Abraham, Jacob, and Moses? Is any link possible?

Some thought not. Two centuries later the fiery church father Tertullian would cry: *What has Athens to do with Jerusalem? What has the Academy to do with the Church? . . . Away with all attempts to produce a Stoic, Platonic, and dialectic Christianity!* [2]

And there were voices in Judaism raised against any attempt to hellenize the faith of Israel. Yet, Philo believed the two must somehow speak with the same voice. He found divine insights in classical literature and great philosophical truths in every page of the Bible.

His problem was how to find a common denominator for Greek and Hebrew thought, a thread he could use to sew together these two vastly different views.

Philo believed Truth is one. He knew the basic insights of Greek thought were true, based on his studies and personal experience. He also knew Judaism and its one God are true as well. Quite reasonably, he deduced that the unspeakably holy Yahweh, the I AM proclaimed by Hebrew Scripture, must be identical with the Logos or Divine Mind of Greek philosophy.

To see one or the other as the only truth was impossible for Philo. Philosophy was too logical, too self-evident, to be false. And for a pious Jew to abandon the God of Israel was unthinkable. Somehow there had to be a key which unlocked the corridor between these two different worlds. But what key? How could a faithful son of Israel find a bridge between the thought-world of Moses and, in Philo's own words, the teachings of *most holy Plato*? [3]

Philo's keen intellect ranged over the vast field of classical studies learned since his boyhood in Alexandria. There, in the works of the great Stoic masters, was the answer. With this key Philo opened the door to modern metaphysical interpretation of the Bible. He single-handedly created the basic method which biblical metaphysicians, such as Charles Fillmore, have employed ever since. And he did it in the first century.

The key is, of course, allegory.

Philo took the techniques of allegory, developed by later Greek schools and especially by the Stoics, and applied the principles to biblical interpretation. An allegory is an explanation of deeper concepts beyond the literal meanings by use of symbolism. When Exodus 3:1 tells us that Moses came to the mountain, we might see a deeper meaning than the event of a prophet climbing a hilltop. It could mean, among other things, that the evolutionary process (Moses)[4] in human consciousness was raised to a higher level, an *exalted state of mind where the divine plan may be perceived and unfolded,*[5] as defined by Charles Fillmore. The possibilities for allegorical interpretation are virtually unlimited.

Philo probably learned the method from the Stoics, a school of philosophy popular in his day, which was based on the teachings of Zeno, issued from his famous painted portico (*stoa* in Greek) at Athens.[6] Zeno had taught harmony with all things, a sort of early divine order, and affirmation of the good in the face of apparent evil. One fragment of his surviving works says: *To live in accordance with nature is to live in accordance with virtue. In doing so, the wise man secures a happy and peaceful course to his own life.*[7]

Zeno lived in the third and fourth centuries B.C., but his teachings became immensely popular by Philo's day and thereafter. Stoics possessed a keen sense of moral uprightness. They might be seen as the forerunners of our own Puritans in their sobriety and overbearing sense of ethical rectitude. As children of the classical Greek culture, Stoics had a real problem with the literature of their religious heritage.

Gods and goddesses of Greek and Roman mythology often behaved in a manner the Stoic saw as scandalous: One deity steals another's wife, begetting illegitimate children by her; another wades into the thick of combat and kills humans for the sheer joy of killing; still others lie, cheat, and steal to obtain their selfish aims.

The noble Stoic rebelled against this sub-human behavior on the part of its divinities. However, rather than cast aside the great literature of Greek civilization (Homer's "Illiad" and "Odyssey" are but two examples), the Stoic developed a method of interpreting religious literature allegorically. Such risqué episodes did not really take place historically, the Stoics assured one another. They are meant to be taken symbolically, representative as they are of deeper, hidden truths. So when the god of war seizes the goddess of beauty, one could see this allegorically as the loss of innocent youth as the soul comes in contact with the struggles of life. For the Stoic, allegory saved the day.

Philo thought so, too. He had great difficulty with a literal reading of many parts of the Jewish Scriptures. Freed from the literal by use of allegory, Philo was able to find common ground for Hellenistic thought on every page of the Torah. In his hands, Moses became the greatest of philosophers, the originator of many truths taught by later Greek thinkers such as Plato. This reading back into the works of venerable old masters the ideas current in one's own time was a practice common to the Platonic school, especially to Middle Platonism of Philo's day. Pagan commentators were doing this in first-century Alexandria. To defend their own Middle

Platonistic doctrines, philosophers reinterpreted Plato and extracted from his words the support they needed.

Philo noted with interest what his pagan contemporaries were doing, deciding that reinterpretation of ancient words was a valid academic enterprise. Dr. David Winston, world-renowned expert on Philo, says that this was just what the philosopher ordered: *Armed with Greek allegorical exegesis (interpretation), which seeks out hidden meanings that lie beneath the surface of any particular text, and given the Middle Platonist... penchant to read back new doctrines into the works of a venerable figure of the past, Philo was fully prepared to do battle for his ancestral tradition.* [8]

And what a battle he fought! Philo's irrepressible energy and vast knowledge produced an endless stream of volumes which blended the best in Hellenism with the eternal verities of the Hebrew faith. His work gained him such prominence in the Jewish world that he lead the delegation to plead the cause of Jews everywhere, taking his argument to the very courtyard of Caesar. Philo's life story is as exciting as his pioneering work in metaphysical writing, so we shall investigate each of them.

Philo wrote so much that a mere sample will have to suffice. The backbone of his work is biblical commentary, which Philo confined to the Torah, or Pentateuch, the first five books of the Hebrew Bible. He wrote much more than this, composing letters, treatises, and whole volumes in defense of Judaism that went beyond biblical commentary. Most of these were sent as one-way communications or have not been preserved because their content did not interest the copyists of later ages. However, what remains of Philo's writings is more than enough to fill several volumes.

It is to biblical commentary Philo returns again and again. He must have considered this his magnum opus—the great lifework of an energetic and devout religionist. Dr. Sandmel explains the way Philo went about his work: *Philo utilizes the supposed meaning of the Hebrew names so as to assign an allegorical entity, and this allegorical entity deals with the names as related to the senses, or the passions, or the mind, or the soul, or to proper logic.*[9]

Philo took the root meanings of the words in a biblical passage and played with them until he found connections between the words of Scripture and the teachings of Plato. Dr. Sandmel assures us he did this in all innocence. *Philo would never have admitted to reading Plato into Scripture; he would have insisted that the Platonism and Stoicism came out of Scripture. He and his Christian successors assert that Philo was right because Plato derived his views from Moses, who was earlier and greater than Plato.*[10]

It is fairly obvious to modern readers that Philo did Platonize Scripture quite extensively, however innocently he proceeded. Yet, all scriptural interpretation is a creative interaction between the words of a long-dead author and the understandings of modern readers. Philo would have probably agreed it is legitimate to "hear" in the words of Scripture messages that the author never intended to convey, for he believed passionately that Truth is one. A work of art or literature may speak to one person with a different voice than it does to another. Perhaps we should not be too critical of him for "Philoizing" Plato after all. And if we do this in modern biblical interpretation, we need to realize it is our creative interaction with the text that produces the best results, even if the author did not have this in mind. As the preface to Unity's *Metaphysical Bible Dictionary* points out: *Our real aim is to assist in leading the student into the inner or spiritual interpretation of the Bible, that he may apply it in the very best and most practical way in his own life. . . . We are always pleased when anyone learns to go within and get his inspiration direct from his own indwelling Lord or Spirit of Truth.*[11]

Philo did just that, and in no haphazard way. His deftness at handling even the most obtrusive scriptural passages is uncanny, yet he has a method to his metaphysics. The commentary moves through allegory after allegory—an endless stream of symbolism—toward what Dr. Sandmel calls the *Grand Allegory.*

Everything in Philo moves majestically toward his goal for all humanity—mystical communion with God. Thus, Philo is a true mystic and not just an abstract speculator. Mysticism is an ancient form of religiosity found in many religious traditions, Western and otherwise. The mystic recognizes no intermediary between himself and God. For him, access to God is always direct and personal. Sometimes this takes the form of meditation, prayer, dance, song, or ecstatic utterance. Mysticism can be the cool reflection of a Catholic priest in his hermitage or the passionate cries and holy dance of Hasidic Jews in the streets of Jerusalem.

The key ingredient in mysticism is involvement by the worshiper directly with God. The mystic is seized by God and, conversely, God is seized by the mystic. Together God and man dance, commune, interact. The aim of all true mysticism is union with God.

This is the key to understanding Philo, for mystical union with God underlies virtually every sentence, every bit of his interpretive dream weaving. Philo deeply believed that Plato and Moses were both teaching ways for humanity to commune with the one true God. He used allegory for mystical and theological purposes, attempting to provide ways for the worshiper to tear down the walls separating man and God. For him, the events of Scripture are intimate, personal happenings in the spiritual lives of everyone. They are parables of individual soul growth.

Nineteen centuries later Charles Fillmore would write: *The fact is that the entire theme of the Bible is man and his various states of mind, represented as persons, tents, tabernacles, temples.*[12]

Truth students who delve into Philo's writings may often find themselves forgetting they were written almost two thousand years ago by a Greek-speaking Jew. Philo frequently uses terms which overlap with language common to Unity literature. His allegory of the patriarchs Enoch and Noah uses exactly the same root meanings as can be found in the *Metaphysical Bible Dictionary*. Enoch represents repentance, and Noah represents tranquillity in both Philo and Fillmore. He speaks of a "higher mystery" and a "lower mystery," which we might call levels of consciousness. He suggests that the soul, upon death, may be reabsorbed into universal consciousness or, in a quaint note reflecting both his openness and his limited astronomical knowledge, he wonders if it might enter a star.[13]

Philo's life was not just the quiet pursuits of a lonely scholar. He was a powerful force in Alexandrian society due to his family's prosperity and his status as a great teacher. Philo's nephew, Alexander, became a Roman general. In Hellenistic society, Jews often rose to high rank and position.

Fortunately Philo did not live to see the

Jews of Palestine rebel against Rome in A.D. 70. The horror of knowing that the Temple had been destroyed by Roman soldiers would have brought double pain to Philo, since his nephew, General Alexander, commanded the Roman forces which took the city.

Philo became a spokesperson for more than just Alexandrian Judaism, drawn as he was into the controversy surrounding the place of Jews in the Empire as a whole. After severe rioting took place during which Jews were killed at Alexandria, Philo led a delegation to Rome to set their position before Caesar and asked for justice and protection under Roman law.

It was Philo's misfortune that these incidents took place during the reign of Emperor Gaius Caligula. Caligula will be remembered as the Emperor who made his horse a member of the Roman senate, who sold the wives and daughters of the senators into public prostitution, and who actually believed he was a god. It was before this megalomaniac that genteel, scholarly Philo presented his case.

Philo tells us what happened during the audience with Caligula. First the Jew-hater Isidorus spoke, ranting about how dangerous and disloyal Philo's people were. Philo and his delegation began to speak in defense of Judaism, but the Emperor seemed more interested in the building project going on around them than the fate of one-tenth of his subjects. Several times during the heat of discussions Caligula jumped up and literally ran out of the room to bark orders in the room next door about the shape of new windows or some other renovation.

Although the debate was supposed to concern the Jews of Alexandria, Philo quickly realized that in the warped mind of the Emperor . . . *the fate of all the Jews everywhere should rest on us five envoys.*[14] In Philo's judgment, the very existence of his people might be at stake. Though a tense encounter, Caligula apparently did not have the presence of mind to follow the debate. At one point in the proceedings, while discussing citizenship of Jews in the Empire, Caligula interrupted them and, in Philo's words, *He put to us this grave and momentous question,* "*Why do you refuse to eat pork*"?[15] Philo decided their cause was in deep trouble.

Fortunately, the quicksilver mind of the Emperor refused to dally with such trivialities as the fate of the Jewish population when important matters like the shape of the windows in his palace had to be decided. Caligula dismissed the case, summarily decreeing that Jews *seem to be people unfortunate rather than wicked*....[16] This ended the audience.

When Caligula was soon murdered by his own people, Philo probably saw it as divine retribution. However, Philo's legation to Caesar did have a positive effect. Jews were eventually afforded full protection under Roman law as long as they did not rebel. They were freed from the requirement to worship the Emperor, a large concession, and from the order to hang graven images of Caesar in their public places such as the temple and synagogues. They were free from compulsory military service, except that a Roman soldier marching by a Jew could lawfully require him to carry the Roman's pack one mile. This is, of course, the background for the teaching of Jesus in Matthew 5:41: "... *and if any one forces you to go one mile, go with him two miles.*" [17]

Philo's legacy in theological circles was profound as well. He opened the doors to metaphysical interpretation of the Bible even before the New Testament was written. He gave us a method of interpretation which allows the creative spirit to flow through those doors even today. Every generation has faced the challenge to reinterpret the Bible and remake the ancient faith in symbolic understandings which would speak to each new age. New insights stream forth as our march toward Christ consciousness presses on down the corridors of history. Philo gave us the key to metaphysical Bible interpretation when he wedded Stoic allegory to Platonic concepts and applied them to the Bible many years ago.

He was an ancient, a devoted Jew, a child of a long-dead classical view. He believed some things which seem very strange to us today. Yet, the basic thread running through the works of Philo Judaeus is mystical/metaphysical.

Philo's methodology never caught on in orthodox Judaism, which continued busily building a wall to shut out foreign influences and preserve its ancient heritage. In all fairness to rabbinic Judaism we must admit that those practices of endogamy, dietary rules, and codes of conduct advocated by the Pharisees did allow Judaism to survive in an increasingly hostile non-Jewish world. Philo was out of step with the hard realities of

Jewish survival and tried to swim upstream against the main current of thought in his community of faith. Hence, Philo has never been very popular among Jewish scholars and commentators.

But Philo lived and died on the edge of another era. There was a new kid on the block among world faiths, a movement sizzling with vitality and eager to share its insights with all humanity, Jew and Gentile alike. It will be a vibrant, new faith springing from Jewish roots which will replant Philo's allegories in the garden of popular religious faith. In this respect we can see Philo as the last great prophet before the coming of Christ, for he lived until the mid-first century and opened doors that Christian scholars would rush through in the generations to come.

Our next study takes us beyond Hellenistic Judaism into contact with a man who has been called the greatest intellectual in church history. It will be Origen, the billiant and controversial North African Christian, who will nurture Philo's arguments beyond their Jewish genesis through to a maturing concept of universalism.

2

Father of
Christian Universalism
Origen
(2d Century A.D.)

The great Philo died about A.D.50, while Paul was just beginning his mission to the Gentiles and before any New Testament book was written. To his dying day Philo remained a staunch advocate of Hellenized Judaism, a true believer in the oneness of Plato's Divine Mind with Yahweh, the God of Israel. Yet the mystical Judaism Philo taught with such passion failed to find favor among the majority of the Jews in the late ancient world. Jewish mysticism would continue as a minority viewpoint within rabbinic Judaism until the flowering of medieval Jewish thought produced one of the most outstanding mystical documents the world has ever known, the "Cabala."

With the destruction of the Temple in A.D. 70 by forces commanded by Philo's own nephew, the apostate Alexander, Judaism became introverted, pessimistic about the world, more concerned with miniscule rulings on every facet of daily life than mystics such as Philo would have wanted. Rabbinic Judaism provided an interpretive mosaic which gave color and depth to everyday life for ordinary Jews living in an increasingly hostile world. During the closing days of the first century and the beginning of the second, that world was to become almost unbearable for the Children of Israel.

Rome drove the Jews from its city precincts in A.D. 90, but the final blow to Jewish optimism came in A.D.132 during the Second Jewish War. The revolt broke out in Jerusalem, led by Simon bar Kocheba. Bar Kocheba was crowned as the Messiah by the illustrious Rabbi Akiba after the rebellion's initial success. The intoxication brought about by freedom from Roman rule led Jerusalem to proclaim the state of Israel reestablished and to strike a coin commemorating

"Simon, Prince of Israel." Dancing in the streets ended abruptly as Rome responded with devastating cruelty and overwhelming might.[18]

Jerusalem fell once more, but this time Roman patience was totally exhausted with rebellion after rebellion from that quarter of their Empire. The entire population of Jerusalem was crucified in brutal reprisal; Roman executioners ran out of wood for crosses and could not find enough level ground to erect all the crosses they had. Roman rule was usually tolerant in regard to religious practices and bitterly cruel in the face of insurrection or armed uprising. The Romans devastated Jerusalem in A.D. 132, built a pagan temple at the site of Solomon's splendid House of the Lord on Mount Zion, and eternally banned any Jew from coming near Jerusalem proper.

One wonders if the words of Jesus might have echoed in the minds of the people involved in this great catastrophe, almost like words of personal advice, given just a century before within the gates of now-ruined Jerusalem: *"But I say to you, Do not resist one who is evil. But if any one strikes you on the right cheek, turn to him the other also . . . Love your enemies and pray for those who persecute you . . . .* " (Matt. 5:39, 44)[19]

As Judaism was retreating behind its cultural walls, the Christian community was reaching out to Hellenistic society with almost reckless abandon. No sector of life was too high or too low for evangelists like St. Paul and his disciples; the second-century church had followed in his footsteps. Women, slaves, freedmen—traditionally lower-status persons in the male-dominated Roman society—became full members of the Christian church, equal to landed gentry or military commanders or even high officials of the government. In its universal appeal, the early Christian church took seriously the words of Paul's letter to the Galatians: *. . . for in Christ Jesus you are all sons of God, through faith. For as many of you as were baptized into Christ have put on Christ. There is neither Jew nor Greek, there is neither slave nor free, there is neither male nor female; for you are all one in Christ Jesus.* (Gal. 3:26-28)[20]

The question yet to be settled was just how should the burgeoning new faith relate to pagan society? Open revolt was foolish and futile, as the sad experience of Simon bar Kocheba had shown. Besides, Christianity had a strongly anti-militant tone in its early days, reflective of the teachings given by Jesus. Two courses seemed open to second-century Christianity: either withdraw from contact with classical civilization or somehow find a bridge between Christian concepts and the best of Greek thought.

Quite a few church fathers opted for the former. After all, wasn't Rome the great Antichrist pictured by John in Revelation, drunk on the blood of the saints? Didn't the Roman emperor seduce the world to idolatry through its loyalty oath, emperor worship? What could the church learn from Aristotle? "What has Athens to do with Jerusalem?" Tertullian asked. Then he launched a diatribe against paganism which ended with these words: *We are but of yesterday, and we have filled every place among you—cities, islands, fortresses, towns, market-places, the very camps, tribes, companies, palace, Senate, and Forum. We have left you only the temples.*[21]

For Tertullian and others, there could be no link between secular learning and the divine revelation of the church. One was of God, the other of the devil. One would prevail, the other would be swept aside in the Judgment Day soon to come.

Down the coast of North Africa an Alexan-

drian Christian scholar battled for his understanding of the ancient faith, too. But his
theology was not the fierce anti-classicism
and intellectual isolationism of Tertullian, it
was the first fully developed Christian
universalism of Origen the classicist.

Origen was an awesome figure in the early
church, a brilliant, passionate, disciplined
man. A compulsive writer and incessant lecturer, his influence is felt to this day in doctrines and concepts of even the most orthodox churches, where he was condemned a
heretic and has remained so for seventeen
hundred years. Origen was a unique personality in world history, a man whose writings
ranged far and wide in an encyclopedic scan
of human knowledge. Treasures, from a man
who was pronounced *anathema* by church
councils soon after his death. Great scholarship and ideas which set the tone for theology
in all the generations to come, yet he was
branded a heretic.

It is his alleged heresies which make Origen
such an interesting person in church history, because a large branch of the Christian
tree has held throughout the centuries
that Origen was right and the so-called orthodox fathers were wrong. So pervasive is the

influence of this early Christian heretic that modern scholars like Catholic theologian Hans Urs Von Balthasar can write: *I know members of religious orders who are praying for the canonization of this martyr and spiritual father of so many saints.*[22] If Origen's ideas had prevailed earlier in the history of the church, a much different form of orthodoxy might have emerged. After all, orthodoxy is just the majority view; it is not necessarily identical with truth. We can recall it was the "orthodox" who stoned the prophets and crucified Jesus.

When we read about Origen, what leaps out of the commentaries and histories of the church are words like *brilliant, genius,* and *towering intellectual giant.* One modern theologian called Origen the Leonardo da Vinci of early Christianity, so vast in scope were his enterprises. Even Origen's long-standing foes have grudgingly admitted that he was probably the most brilliant mind of the early church, perhaps the keenest intellect in the entire history of Christianity. Standing beside such monumental personages as Augustine, Aquinas, and Luther, that is quite a compliment.

Yet, Origen's brainpower alone hardly

would have left such a deep mark on the church had not his intellect been matched by a tremendous, productive scholarship and a passionate personal piety, a piety that would reach excesses in his quest for ascetic purity.

His creativity was boundless. He wrote a mountain of books, so many that even a hardy soul like St. Jerome groaned, *"Has anyone read everything that Origen wrote?"*[23] Origen's biblical commentaries alone are so vast that none has survived in its entirety. Jerome claims that Origen wrote six thousand books, a number no doubt inflated by ancient exuberance. However, if we apply a decimal point to the figure to allow for Jerome's enthusiasm, that would still leave Origen with six hundred books to his credit, an accomplishment unmatched by any other author in Christian history.

In his unbridled passion for learning, Origen became the first true biblical scholar of our Christian heritage. He learned Hebrew so he could study the Jewish Scriptures in the original language, and tradition has it that he discoursed at length with rabbis about the meanings of Hebrew words and phrases. According to one of his admirers, his pupil, the church historian Eusebius, Origen even found some ancient biblical manuscripts in a jar at Jericho. Thus, in a way, he prefigured modern biblical archaeology and the discovery of the Dead Sea scrolls.[24]

He lived the life of an ascetic, one devoted to spiritual growth through strict discipline and denying the body its natural desires. He slept on the floor, ate no meat, drank no wine, had only one coat and no shoes. When Origen was seventeen, he urged his father to accept martyrdom, avoiding that fate himself only because his mother hid the young boy's clothes and wouldn't let him out of the house.

Today, some people may see his actions as obsessive or compulsive: he worked far into the night, denied himself all but the scantest sleep, and almost surely castrated himself so as to remove from his life sexual temptation and the merest hint of scandal. His death in A.D. 250 came after imprisonment and extensive torture for the "crime" of being a Christian. Origen's torturers marveled at how heroically he endured his last ordeal. They released him, but he died soon afterward. He was sixty-six.

It is difficult for us, perched at the edge of the twenty-first century, to comprehend the forces that motivated these ascetics of early

Christianity. Some of them went off into the
desert to live atop pillars for the rest of their
lives; others held their hands upraised in
penance for some imagined sin until their
joints froze in place. Men whipped themselves with cords, mutilated themselves,
fasted until they were near death. In this environment, Origen was almost a moderate.
He never intended that his personal asceticism was to become the norm for anyone else.
Whatever terrible internal needs drove him to
self-mutilation and denial of the good of this
world are certainly not reflected in his work,
which is a masterpiece of logic, cool-headed-
ness, and deep love for God.

As we look at the works of Origen we might
do well to recall that he lived in a world we
shall never fully understand, a brutal and
oppressive world which was beginning to
crumble around him. The fall of Rome was
still centuries away, but the cracks had
already begun to show at the edges of the
Empire which would soon spread to metro-
politan Rome itself. Certainly, excesses like
Origen practiced are not regarded as healthy
religious impulses today; but Origen does not
live today. It is always a danger in studying
our ancestors in the ancient faith—be they

Origen, Emerson, or even Fillmore—to project backward our values and scientific understandings upon men and women of earlier generations. For the purposes of a historical appraisal, we need to let them be who they were. They understood Truth at their level, and so we strive to do the same today. Our vision of Truth is ours; Origen's was his. We can certainly learn from him as we discover Truths for the modern age. His vision can be our inspiration.

And what was Origen's vision? Dr. Rowan A. Greer of Yale Divinity School describes Origen's great hope, the historical/mystical dream he had for the faith of Jesus: *Specifically, he saw the Christian hope not as an alternative to the Roman world, but as the catalyst that could rescue and transform what was best in it. His theology was an attempt to translate the Gospel into a language intelligible to the pagan, especially the thoughtful and educated pagan.*[25]

It was Origen's all-consuming passion for this vision—his hope that Christ could save Hellenistic culture from decay and ruin—that drove him beyond moderation to asceticism and eventually to death as a martyr. For him Christianity was not merely the Truth, it was the only hope for a world disintegrating before his eyes. With such a background, perhaps we can forgive him some of his excesses. The contribution Origen made to Western thought is unparalleled in world history.

He became the first fully competent philosopher/theologian to think through the Christian teachings and devise a systematic theology that spoke to the mind as well as the heart. In doing so he unintentionally provoked a controversy which still rages in Christendom, although the passing centuries have rendered the Origenist position triumphant in Christian theological circles of higher thought. Three ideas he gave us are worthy of considering in specific details: his *Christology* or theology of the nature and person of Jesus, his concept of universal salvation or *universalism,* and his use of *allegory* to interpret the Bible after the manner begun by Philo Judaeus. In all three categories, we shall discover a long-lost relative to modern metaphysical Christianity in the ideas of this ancient genius and church father. Origen himself would have approved of an open-minded approach to his works. He wrote: *If anyone can find something better and can confirm what he says by clear proofs from Holy*

Scripture, let his opinion be preferred to ours.[26]

In this spirit, Origen set off on some of the most original theological thinking Western humanity would ever encounter. And nothing points the way clearer in Origen's thought than his *Christology,* in which Origen related his beliefs about the nature and person of Jesus.

Origen believed that Jesus of Nazareth was the earthly manifestation of the *Divine Mind* or *Logos.* He saw Jesus Christ as preexistent, that is, having lived before incarnation in this world as Jesus of Nazareth. For Origen, Jesus the Christ was a being of impeccable character and spirituality whom Divine Mind chose for the mission of bringing salvation to all God's children. Origen believed Jesus was so thoroughly in harmony with God that to see Jesus was to know what God is like. In this regard, Origen foreshadowed twentieth-century thinkers of the neoorthodox school such as Swiss theologian Karl Barth.

In his classic series "A History of Christian Thought," Arthur Cushman McGiffert described Origen's Christology: *The divine Logos could not directly assume a human body, the unlikeness between them being too*

*great. He therefore united with one of the cre-
ated spirits who by his preeminent virtue had
proved himself worthy of the honor. This
spirit, joined to the divine Logos, took on a
human body, thus becoming a human soul,
and advanced step by step until he attained
complete divinity.*[27]

For Origen, Christ consciousness was attained, not ordained. Although his mythology of a preexistent match between a human
soul and the Divine Mind may not reflect the
beliefs of modern metaphysical Christians,
we can clearly see he was a freethinker who
paved the way for the belief in preexistence,
reincarnation, and Christ consciousness.
When Origen was condemned, it was his
belief in preexistence of souls which church
councils stiffly pronounced *anathema* or ac-
cursed. This closed the door to a belief in reincarnation also, since preexistence of a soul is
logically required for that soul to reincarnate
in this world. Origen also leaned toward
Unity's definition of the trinity as mind, idea,
and expression, although he never expressed
it exactly this way. He held that the Father is
eternally generating the Son, and that all created souls are in some mystical way one with
this one Power. Origen goes as far as saying

that the Logos is the Father in the same way that a thought represents its thinker: Mind and idea are somehow one.[28] It would take metaphysicians centuries to sort this out, but Origen held a beacon in the darkness by which many mystics to come would find their way.

Universalism was Origen's belief that all would be saved. He was unequivocal on this, insisting that any belief in eternal punishment was unworthy of the God of Jesus. Origen repeatedly insisted that the "wrath of God" is not some emotional outburst on the part of Divine Mind, but a series of natural consequences and built-in "punishments" which teach, purify, and uplift the soul in its quest for holiness. He was sure that terms like *heaven, hell, resurrection,* and the *Second Coming* had symbolic meanings that far transcended any crude literalism. He taught that everyone would be saved because God is not demented, and it would take a demented deity to punish anyone for all eternity. When his opponents fired back that his theology could mean that even the devil would be saved, Origen agreed. (No wonder they declared him a heretic!) He was the father of Christian universalism, an unyielding believer in divine goodness.

Allegory was Origen's mystical interpretation of biblical symbolism. Origen held that there is a threefold meaning in Scripture that corresponds to the threefold division he saw in human nature: body, soul, and spirit, which equates to literal, moral, and spiritual. George W. Anderson discusses Origen's biblical interpretation in his article on the "History of Biblical Interpretation:" *The literal sense is what is understood by the ordinary, unenlightened Christian. The higher senses, the moral and spiritual, are appropriate to those further advanced in understanding and insight, though none can fathom the ultimate divine mystery concealed in scripture.*[29]

And is literalism valid? Origen grudgingly said yes, it is valid for those at that level of understanding. But such absurdities as the creation account in Genesis I where three "days" pass before the sun, moon, and the stars are formed cannot be taken literally unless one dips into illogic. Anderson continues describing the Origenist view: *Such difficult or offensive elements in the text were put there by God to incite the reader to search for the higher meanings. The moral sense is related not only to duty and obedience but to the entire range of the soul's experience. The spiritual sense conveys the divine nature and purpose.*[30]

Here Origen is reaching for a way to release deeper meanings from the treasure house of the Scriptures. Following in Philo's footsteps, he is a true son of the Alexandrian school of biblical interpretation, which was allegorical and mystical rather than slavishly literal. Whereas Tertullian would cry, "I believe it because it is absurd," Origen would shake his head and sigh, "We must see whether it is not possible to find a more worthy interpretation for these passages."[31]

Writing as he did on the eve of the fall of Rome, Origen's work is a vast series of affirmations, in theological language, proclaiming the goodness of God and the perfectability of humanity. When voices were being raised within Christianity to wall off Christian thought from the rest of human experience, Origen sounded his trumpet call for universalism in thought and deed. He believed in the capacity of us, his brothers and sisters throughout humanity's ages to come, to find Truth through following our own indwelling spirit of Truth. Clearly, his words ring down the corridors of time as though he were writing for us when he said: *We see, therefore, that men have a blood-kinship with God . . . it is possible that a rational mind also, by advancing from a knowledge of small to a knowledge of greater things and from things visible to things invisible, may attain to an increasingly perfect understanding.* [32]

Origen is universally proclaimed the greatest genius of the early church. In much of his teaching, he was a direct predecessor to modern metaphysical Christianity.

Why, then, did a dark cloud loom over the sunny optimism of the early church? What kept Origenism from spreading the good news of universal salvation to the ends of the earth and brought instead the bad news of human sinfulness? To this question we shall now turn our attention.

3

Free Will or Predestination? Pelagius, Augustine, and Hypatia (5th Century A.D.)

The fifth century of our Christian Era saw one age ending and another beginning. Ancient civilization, the world of classical Greek creativity and impetuous curiosity, collapsed and died of old age, while the medieval period, shrouded in superstition and cowed by fears of hellfire, was just being born. It was a transition period for western civilization, a bottleneck between two worlds, much like our own time. As with any turbulent period, contrasting prevalent forces pulled at fifth-century people from several directions at once, creating tremendous tension at the center of life.

It was the sort of age William Butler Yeats described:

> *Things fall apart; the center cannot hold;*
> *Mere anarchy is loosed upon the world,*
> *The blood-dimmed tide is loosed, and*
>   *everywhere*
> *The ceremony of innocence is drowned.*
> *The best lack all conviction, while the*
>   *worst*
> *Are full of passionate intensity.*[33]

And from this furious commotion the leaders of the Church were not exempt. Christianity, no longer a persecuted minority, now held sway as the only lawful religious faith of the Empire. Only in the countryside surrounding the great cities did paganism maintain its hold on the people, and these were illiterates who clung tenaciously to ancestral traditions in fear of new ideas. In fact, the word *pagan* comes from the Latin *paganus*, or "country-dweller."

At the heart of late-ancient civilization, the triumph of Christianity was complete. Or was it?

Certainly, the official religion of the Roman world was now the faith of Jesus. After centuries of sporadic persecutions, one would expect the leaders of Christianity to understand the needs of the oppressed and allow for religious tolerance within the crumbling remains of Roman civilization now that the Church was supreme. They did not. When Christian orthodoxy became the only lawful religion of the Empire, its leaders busily set to work oppressing, harassing, and killing the pagans and, even more incredibly, persecuting other Christians who did not conform to orthodox beliefs.

Weakened though it might be from internal decay, Rome was still strong enough to torture her own people for religious nonconformity. But now the orthodox Christians held the whips and drove the pagans or heretical Christians into hiding. It was a sad departure from the spirit of ancient Christianity and the teachings of Jesus Christ.

Medieval Christianity would become a repressive catacomb where isolated intellectuals secluded themselves to rethink the message of Jesus but where the rank-and-file Christian was held in serfdom to a system of religious and political oppression that controlled his life in both this world and the world to come. Every age has produced its great thinkers, and medieval Europe was no exception, as we shall see when we look at people like John Scotus Erigena and Meister Eckehart. In fact, it is the task of theology to rethink and reshape the Christian message for each succeeding generation. That is precisely what the founders of Unity, Charles and Myrtle Fillmore, did for their generation. Historian Paul Johnson contends that there really never has been a universal agreement on what the Christian faith teaches. There have been sects, schisms, and "new thought" movements from the very beginnings of the faith. Any of these could have captured the "orthodox" position and become a central belief of Christianity.[34] Most, however, remained a part of the harmony of the church rather than becoming the melody line.

In the early fifth century, two melodies were vying for centrality in the developing medieval symphony. The one that emerged victorious was a sad tune, indeed. It told of the evil nature of humankind, the need for hellfire to keep the unruly passions of unregenerate man in his place. It sang of salvation, but only for the few, the elect, and it chanted in somber tones of the total inability of humans to do anything of value because of

our total depravity as children of Adam, born
in original sin.

For the majority of medieval Christian
thinkers, everything human was corrupt; the
natural state of human consciousness was
full rebellion against God. The natural destination for all humankind was a quick flight
through life toward our richly merited damnation. At the end of life, Jesus waited, usually painted sitting on a rainbow with a sword
coming out of one ear and a lily out of the
other. Jesus would judge the soul according
to a preordained, predestined roster of the
saved and the damned. A few chosen souls
would wing their way to eternal bliss in
heaven; the vast majority of human spirits
would fall into the abyss to be tortured with
Satan for all eternity.

This was the worldview of the medieval
church. It was Christianity at its worst, most
unhealthy expression, perhaps the most pessimistic, pathological theology our world has
ever produced. Yet, it didn't have to go the
way it did. Paul Johnson comments: *The
story might have been different. There were
elements in Christianity at the beginning of
the fifth century striving to create a distinctive Christian higher culture on Origenist*

lines. Their frustration and destruction was very largely the work of one man ... Augustine was the dark genius of imperial Christianity, the ideologue of the Church-State alliance, and the fabricator of the medieval mentality. [35]

These "elements in Christianity ... striving to create a distinctive Christian higher culture on Origenist lines" chose to rally around a most unlikely controversialist, a pious soul who lived the Church and despised discord, a moderate ascetic who thought love and reason would carry Truth to victory—the British monk Pelagius. Although Pelagianism carries the stigma of heresy and Pelagius has been called the heresiarch, or father of heresy, a fresh look at the issues from more modern perspectives may show otherwise. Johnson writes: ... *certainly, if we contrast his philosophy with Paul's, it can be seen that Augustine, not Pelagius, was the heresiarch —the greatest of them all in terms of his influence.* [36]

Augustine represented the darker, pessimistic, predestinarian position. Pelagius represented the sunny, optimistic theology of free will and human potential. Even a superficial study of the Pelagian Controversy, as it

is called in church history, shows that
modern metaphysical Christianity owes a
great debt to Pelagius, who is another of our
unsung heroes of the ancient faith.

The combatants drew their battle lines
along three general questions: what is the
essential nature of humanity—good or evil?
Is there freedom to choose or are we predestined either to salvation or damnation?
(The term for this was "irresistible grace.")
And most crucially, can a person do good on
his own, or does all virtue depend on God's
initiative? In other words, does a person have
the power to do good without God forcing the
good deed upon him? Augustine said no; Pelagius said yes. The issue was therefore clear-
cut and unmistakable.

Pelagius was concerned with morality and
ethics. He saw Augustine's emphasis on the
inability of depraved humanity to do anything good as an excuse to avoid moral responsibility. If a man cannot act morally, if
keeping God's rules is beyond him, why then
should he struggle to be a good person? If
people are predestined to heaven or hell, what
difference does it make how we treat our
neighbors in the here and now?

The monstrous absurdity that God damns

and blesses whomsoever He chooses, regardless of their efforts or character, seemed subhuman to Pelagius, let alone sub-Christian. He reasoned that we must be able to do good or the whole concept of good and evil is useless. One of his strongest supporters, Coelsestrius, capsulized the argument in a fine piece of classical logic: *Again, it is to be inquired whether a man ought to be sinless. Without a doubt, he ought. And if a man ought, he can; if he cannot he ought not. And if a man ought not be sinless then he ought to be sinful, and that will not be sin which it is admitted he ought to do.*[37]

Augustine was not impressed. For him, there was ample evidence in the world for his belief in total depravity and preordained damnation/salvation. Physical death and suffering were but two examples of divine retribution visited upon all humanity for the sin of Adam. Augustine believed we are born in original sin, which he unhesitatingly identified with the act of sexual reproduction. All humanity is fatally flawed because when Adam sinned the human race fell from grace to total rebellion against God, hence death, suffering, sickness, and pain.

Pelagius replied that death is natural, not

the result of the "fall of Adam." Death is a result of being born finite and would have happened anyway, he said, even if Adam had not sinned. All humans have free choice, just as Adam did. Anything less would be unworthy of the Creator and Father of Jesus Christ, the God of love and justice.[38]

Augustine and the medieval church after him insisted that humans sin because their basic nature is corrupt: people sin because they are sinners. Pelagius countered that human nature is neither wholly corrupt nor wholly perfect, yet it is free. Freedom means the ability to choose good or evil; it means that total depravity is nonsense, and spiritual perfection comes a bit later in the program. Pelagius turned the Augustinian formula around: people are sinners because they sin. We might say, people are imperfect because they are still working on their perfection.

For Pelagius and the Pelagians, people are not born thieves but become thieves by stealing, which is an act of free choice. And, he reasoned, if it is a free choice to sin then we must be free to be perfect, too. Pelagius admitted that perfection was rare, but insisted it was possible. Is this not, he asked, what

Jesus meant when He commanded: "... *be perfect, as your heavenly father is perfect*"? (Matt. 5:48) [39]

At first Augustine and his party, which included the brilliant but disparaging Saint Jerome, treated Pelagius with utmost respect. Well known as a pious, erudite soul whose character was above reproach, Augustine initially seemed a bit embarrassed that he had differences of opinion with Pelagius. As late as A.D. 413 he sent the British monk, who then resided at Rome, a courteous letter. The real break between them occurred a year later. It was prompted by an event so minor that we only know about it because it proved a pivotal point in the Pelagian controversy.

Demetrias, daughter of a wealthy Roman gentleman, decided to take the veil as a virgin, the early Christian term for those whom we call nuns. She was living at Carthage when she embarked on this new vocation, but her Roman mother wanted the event celebrated throughout the Empire. She solicited and received lengthy essays of advice for her daughter from well-known contemporary divines, among them Jerome and Pelagius.

Jerome got a copy of Pelagius' letter and was so outraged he brought it to the attention of his friend, the Bishop of Hippo, Augustine. Augustine read the letter, agreeing with Jerome's evaluation. In fact, he thought the treatise so dangerous he felt compelled to warn the mother of Demetrias about its doubtful orthodoxy.[40] The letter, which may seem innocent enough to us, nevertheless contained the following passage which infuriated Augustine: *Whenever I have to speak concerning moral instruction and holy living I am accustomed to point out first the force and quality of human nature and what it is able to accomplish and then to incite the mind of the hearer to many kinds of virtue, since it is not without profit to be summoned to those things which perhaps he had assumed are impossible to him. For we are by no means able to tread the way of virtue unless we have hope as a companion.*[41]

This seemingly innocuous exhortation to virtuous living angered Augustine because he considered it sacrilegious to speak of human nature as able to accomplish anything. Jerome, best known for his translation of the Bible into the Latin Vulgate, called Pelagius a "corpulent dog," shouting that Pelagianism was a dangerous heresy.

Yet Pelagius was acquitted by a synod of

Palestinian bishops in 415. His position was by far more popular than the pessimism of the North Africans under the lead of Augustine. Pelagianism was not only popular, it was an ancient viewpoint, as Johnson points out: *Pelagius was not an isolate heretic. He represented the ordinary doctrine of people who were educated in Greek thinking, especially in Stoic traditions, and for whom freedom is the essential nature of man.*[42]

Augustine would not relent. He hounded Pelagius and his followers across the length of the Empire. He had them twice declared heretical at synods in North Africa. He wrote volumes against Pelagianism. Finally, he was able to get the whole affair before the Bishop of Rome, Pope Zosimus.

The Holy See inclined toward Pelagius, who had the support of several rich and powerful Roman families. The African faction pressed for Pelagianism to be declared heretical. Zosimus waivered, hesitated. He clearly did not want to rule on this. With so many influential people on both sides, he was bound to infuriate someone, and perhaps even provoke a major split in the church.

Johnson says the North Africans grew impatient. Finally, Augustine's party resorted to outright bribery: *Eighty fine Numidian stallions, bred on episcopal estates in Africa, were shipped to Italy and distributed among the imperial cavalry commanders whose squadrons, in the last resort, imposed Augustine's theory of grace. To the imperial authorities, the Pelagians were represented as disturbers of the public peace ....*[43]

What theology could not accomplish by argument, imperial power established through the force of arms. Zosimus reluctantly issued a formal condemnation of Pelagius in 418. It was a sad commentary on the direction the so-called orthodox church was taking.

Yet it was not by the force of his personality alone, nor the machinations of his political allies, that Augustine defeated optimistic Pelagianists. An event occurred just as the controversy gathered which overshadowed all happenings in fifth-century Europe. It was a calamity so profound that Augustine's developing theory of human total depravity made sense when seen in the light of this world-shattering cataclysm.

In 411 Alaric the Goth captured and sacked the city of Rome. The eternal city, which Tertullian had believed would last until

Judgment Day, had fallen.

Saint Jerome in far-off Bethlehem pushed aside his translation of the Bible to cry out in anguish: *The entire human race is implicated in the catastrophe. My voice is choked, and my words are broken with sobs while I write:* Capitur urbs quae totum cepit orbem. *(The city is now taken that once held the world.)* [44]

Augustine watched these events from the safety of North Africa. Even though he could not know that his own region would soon fall to barbarian invasions and he would die in the siege of Hippo, Augustine was troubled, too. Could there be any better evidence that his position was the true one—that man was evil, corrupt—than this world-toppling event? He took paper and pen and wrote: *The city of God endureth forever, though the greatest city on earth is fallen....* [45]

Rome, he decided, was the city of man, whose creations would always be tainted by sin. The Church, on the other hand, was the "City of God," a divine kingdom which would never fall. It was these events which prompted him to write his greatest work by that title. He hammered away at this theme for the rest of his life, and in a world where the foundations shook and people cried for some sort of stability, indeed this was a comforting theme. Perhaps more than anything, the fall of Rome sealed the doom of Pelagian optimism and opened the dark doorway to medieval oppression, fear, and pessimism.

Everything from classical civilization became suspect, for did it not represent the city of man, the kingdom of Satan? One case which sadly showed this gathering gloom was Hypatia of Alexandria. The city of Philo and Origen, even in that bastion of ancient liberalism, reactionary forces grew strong in the fifth century. Fanaticism moved quickly to attack anyone with classical learning, like Hypatia possessed.

Hypatia was an extraordinary woman. We have a contemporary account of her accomplishments written by the Christian historian Socrates. She was a brilliant scholar with credentials in literature and the sciences. She was the curator of the great classical museum of Alexandria, a research and teaching facility unmatched in the ancient world. Daughter of the philosopher Theon, Hypatia was reputed to be the finest philosopher of her time.

As a Platonist, she fell into the general school of thought which informed Philo,

Clement, Origen, and many of our "fathers" in the ancient faith, although she was not a Christian. That, more than anything, was her great crime in the eyes of the fanatical street rabble of Alexandria who claimed to be followers of Jesus.

Historian Socrates writes of her: *... she explained all the principles of philosophy to her auditors. Therefore many from all sides, wishing to study philosophy, came to her. On account of the self-possession and ease of manner which she had acquired by her study, she not infrequently appeared with modesty in the presence of magistrates. Neither did she feel abashed in entering an assembly of men. For all men, on account of her extraordinary dignity and virtue, admired her all the more.* [46]

By all unbiased reports, Hypatia was a superior person. Any other time in history she might be remembered for her academics, her philosophical achievements, and her virtue. Instead, she became a martyr to the demise of classical civilization. In 415 a fanatical mob, stirred up against her by Saint Cyril, the local bishop, waylaid her on the way home. Socrates tells the unpleasant story: *Dragging her from her carriage they*

*took her to the church called Caesareum.
There they completely stripped her and
murdered her with tiles ... This affair
brought no little opprobrium (disgrace), not
only upon Cyril but upon the whole Alexandrian Church.*[47]

Socrates expressed horror at this act,
which was to become painfully frequent as
medieval fears and heresy-hunting took the
place of early Christian enthusiasm and
universalism. He summarized: *And surely
murders, fights, and actions of that sort are
altogether alien to those who hold the things
of Christ.*[48]

It was Augustine who provided the ratio-
nale for state persecution and torture of heretics. One cannot help but wonder what might
have been the course of Western civilization
if Pelagius, not Augustine, had prevailed.
Perhaps the world was not ready yet for
Pelagianism. Perhaps human consciousness
was not at a level to accept responsibility for
its actions in an atmosphere of freedom.
Perhaps the people of that long-dead era were
like frightened children playing at the edge of
night, terrorized by the shapes of shadows
and not knowing how to find the light switch
that would turn darkness to day, even though

Jesus had told them, *"You are the light of the world."*

Certainly, people like Pelagius and Hypatia are examples of humanity at its best. But even Augustine, who gave us such a heritage of pessimism, also gave us a goal to strive toward. He ardently wished that each believer might come into direct communion with God, as his "Confessions," his spiritual autobiography, so clearly shows. A child of his age, Augustine never intended that his teachings should lead to the Dark Ages or become the proof-texts for the great terror of the Inquisition. The group consciousness of medieval humanity took it in that direction against his good intent.

Augustine, Pelagius, and Hypatia represented three vastly different worldviews and yet each has contributed to modern mystical/metaphysical Christianity. It would take centuries for Origen's universalism and Pelagian optimism to capture center stage in Christian theology. However, today this is the case. Virtually all modern theologians, outside the fundamentalist fringe, accept Origen's teaching that none shall be damned forever, and Pelagius' insistence on individual free will. The victory of Pelagianism's theology of hope over Augustinian gloom and doom could have come sooner if the church had read and studied its mystical theologians.

In our first three studies of the ancestors to practical Christianity, we have explored the teachings of a few fathers of the faith: Philo, Origen, and Pelagius. Now we turn to the medieval period to look at some Christian thinkers whom I call the "Marvelous Medieval Mystics." We shall look at the works of a Christian philosopher (John Scotus Erigena) and a preacher/teacher whose mysticism is still popular reading, Meister Eckehart. First we must dig a little deeper and strike the foundation-stone for all medieval and subsequent mystical writings in the Christian culture, the great father of mysticism in the Western world, Dionysius the Areopagite. His influence is enormous, and yet few people outside academic Christian circles have heard of him. Truth students may find much to cheer about as we look at this unknown soldier of the ancient faith.

Part II

Those Marvelous Medieval Mystics

4

Brightness of the Divine Darkness Pseudo-Dionysius the Areopagite (c. 5th Century A.D.)

One of the many surprises a student of religious studies will encounter early in his career is that many books claim to be written by someone other than the actual author. Large numbers of books, letters, and treatises which assert themselves to be from the hand of a well-known figure are in fact from the pen of an unknown author writing much later under a pen name.

In fact, this method of pseudonymous writing was widely practiced in classical civilization. One historian writes: *What seems to us now a falsification was a custom in ancient writing. It was not a betrayal in any technical or moral sense to launch one's books under famous names.*[49]

There is ample evidence that quite a few biblical books, for example, were not written by the persons the church has traditionally assumed wrote them. We have known for almost a hundred years that Moses could not have written the Torah (first five books of the Bible). And although ministers who graduate from mainline Protestant or Catholic theological seminaries are well aware of this, such an idea is still a glaring shock in many corners of Christianity.

Most students of Unity are fascinated rather than shocked when they learn that the Gospels were not written by the apostles and that probably half the letters of Paul were actually written by his disciples years after his martyrdom. However, this idea is so disturbing to some people that some clergymen seldom reveal what their seminary professors taught them years ago.

If the practice of pseudonymous writing was so widespread, a natural question occurs to the modern mind: Why did so many books get mislabeled? Was there intentional deceit? The answer is yes and no. Sometimes the intent was deceitful, and sometimes it was not.

Early Christianity seethed with new energy like a bubbling, creative cauldron. Most of the preaching and teaching came not through written means but by the spoken word. Sometimes a Christian teacher would write down his thoughts or the thoughts of his mentor. Paul frankly admits that his writings are much more effective than his physical presence (II Cor. 10), and he commands that his readers should find copies of his letters to other churches and read them, too. (Col. 4:16)

As these writings became more available, the new Christian "books" began to find use as Scripture beside the Jewish Bible. So to support one's ideas, it was important that a viewpoint representing your theology made it into the category of "sacred scripture." Often, followers of major teachers such as Paul, James, John, and Peter set down ideas they believe their masters would have taught. They borrowed this method from common practice in Hellenistic (Greco-Roman) civilization.

Hundreds of years before, Plato had done the same. Using his mentor, Socrates, as the main character, Plato wrote his great

Dialogues. Thus the "Dialogues of Plato" are really the dialogues of Socrates. Or are they? Plato wrote them from his ideas of what Socrates taught.

Several New Testament authors did the same. Some wrote in Paul's name (Ephesians, I and II Timothy, Titus, and perhaps others). Some wrote "According to" other disciples (Matthew, II Peter, John). Some never claimed to be the work of an apostle but were later attributed to a disciple of Jesus by church tradition (Mark, Luke in Acts, Hebrews, James, and Jude).

More surprising for newcomers to church history, there are scores of books from the early Christian period (through A.D. 200) that did not make it into the canon of the New Testament and yet claimed to be from the hands of apostles. To name just a few: the Gospels of Thomas, Peter, Phillip, and Ebionites; the Acts of John, Peter, Paul, Andrew, Thomas; the Teaching of the Apostles (Didache); the Letters of Pilate, Lentulus, Barnabas, and the Apostles; the Martyrdom of Matthew; the Infancy Gospels—the list could go on.[50] They are believed by the overwhelming majority to be forgeries.

Generally, the early church could tell the difference between a spiritually solvent work like Ephesians (written by an admirer of Paul, probably near the end of the first century) and works like the Infancy narratives (in which young Jesus curses children who subsequently die). There were, however, many good samples of early Christian writing (like the Shepherd of Hermas and the Didache) which nevertheless did not find their way into the New Testament.

Even so, authors continued to use names of apostles and great figures from the first century to add validity to their ideas and authority to their works. In the fifth century a series of writings appeared which purported to flow from the pen of Dionysius, an early follower of the Apostle Paul, who received a one-line mention in the New Testament: *But some men joined him and believed, among them Dionysius the Areopagite.* (Acts 17:34) [51]

These writings soon gained immense popularity and were widely held to be genuine works of the apostolic age. Dr. Paul Tillich discussed this mistake in his book, "A History of Christian Thought": *Dionysius the Areopagite is the classic Christian mystic, one of the most interesting figures in Eastern church history. He was also of extreme importance in the West. In Acts 17:34 we read of a man called Dionysius who followed Paul after he had preached in the Areopagus (the famous Mars' Hill sermon). His name was used by a writer who lived around A.D. 500. In the tradition this man was accepted as the real Dionysius who talked with Paul.... It is an established historical fact that the man who wrote these books wrote around A.D. 500 and used the name of Paul's companion in Athens in order to lend authority to his books.*[52]

Pseudo-Dionysius, whoever he was, brought a sunburst of light to the leading edge of the dark ages. All medieval and modern mysticism to come afterward has been directly or indirectly affected by this lone author. Laboring in secret at his desk, he wrestled with concepts like Divine Mind, the Silence, and the one Power and Presence, which he had the foresight to glean from the pages of the Gospels.

While the rest of Christianity amused itself by nit-picking about the nature and person of Jesus (the Christological Controversies), Dionysius soared like a lonely eagle above these squabbles to reach for mystical union with God. His goal was Christ-consciousness, and his method was prayer and meditation on the unspeakable goodness of God. He wrote: *Wherefore, it is above all necessary, especially in theology, to begin with prayer, not in order to attract to ourselves the power which is present everywhere and nowhere, but by commemorating and calling upon God to give ourselves into his hands and become one with him.* [53]

Historian Arthur Cushman McGiffert observed that Dionysius' attitude was wholly unlike that of his day. He writes: *The contrast between his spirit and that of many other theologians of the age, is shown by his sixth letter addressed to the presbyter Sosipater, in which he exhorts him not to attack those that differ with him but to set forth the truth and let it speak for itself.* [54]

Where other early medieval churchmen heaped scorn and pronounced anathemas on their opponents, Dionysius urged Christians to refrain from attack thoughts and let Truth stand as its own defense. In this way he anticipated the spirit of modern practical Christianity. Charles Fillmore later echoed Dionysius' sentiments in *Talks on Truth: Love does not brag about its demonstrations.*

It simply lives the life, and lets its works speak for it.[55]

Our affinities with these pseudonymous fifth-century writings run far deeper than this. Except for his flowery style and complicated mythologies about angelic hierarchies, much of what Dionysius wrote could have come from the pages of *Lessons in Truth* or from class notes taken during lectures on metaphysics as taught at Unity Village.

As each "new" idea finds its way into mystical Christianity of the modern age, be it the message of a "Jonathan Livingston Seagull," the insights of "Handbook to Higher Consciousness," or the self-study in Platonism of "A Course in Miracles," we would do well to look backward to the long course of Christian thought which contains the germ of most allegedly new realizations. Dionysius is a case in point. Writing fifteen hundred years ago, he taught some ideas which we have erroneously labeled "New Thought." Some of those ancient teachings include: one Power and Presence, God, the good omnipotent; nonexistence of evil as a power or force; the impersonal nature of God; the goal of all life is Christ-consciousness and union with the Divine; mysticism as the highest form of knowledge; the Silence (he did not use the term but taught the concept, calling it "the super-essential brightness of the divine darkness"); metaphysical biblical interpretation and the use of allegory; the importance of prayer; everything we say about God is symbolic, since He is beyond comprehension or beyond human categories like good and perfection; God is beyond the physical universe (hence, metaphysical); God is present everywhere (hence, personal); and all paths lead to God, but some lead more directly than others.

We cannot hope to give adequate space to cover each metaphysical "friend" in detail. However, even a brief look at such innovators as Dionysius would not be complete without at least a fleeting glance at some of his more interesting doctrines. So let us take a moment to explore four areas opened up to mystical Christianity by this long-ago pioneer. We shall study his teaching on the one Power and Presence, belief in the nonexistence of evil, views on the impersonal nature of God, and symbolic theology.

As we look at the works of Dionysius, we need to remind ourselves that these ideas came from the mind of a Christian writer a millenium and a half ago. And nowhere is the timeless quality of his ideas more evident than in his teaching about the absolute omnipotence and omnipresence of God.

1. *One Power/One Presence.* Along with the divinity of each individual, the concept of the one Power/Presence is perhaps the central teaching of modern metaphysical Christianity. While Dionysius did not explicitly mention the divinity of man, he certainly implied it. But, let him speak for himself as he gives testimony to the one Power and Presence, God, the good: ... *Hence all Being, all Power, all Activity, all Condition, all Perception, all Reason, all Intuition, all Apprehension, all Understanding, all Communion—in a word, all that is—comes from the Beautiful and Good, hath its very existence in the Beautiful and Good, and turns toward the Beautiful and Good. Yea, all that exists and that comes into being, exists and comes into being because of the Beautiful and Good; and unto this Object all things gaze and by It are moved and conserved, and for the sake of It, because of It and in It, existeth every originating Principle.*[56]

Could there be a more cogent statement of the all-present, all-powerful nature of God?

Dionysius goes on to quote Romans 11:36 as scriptural evidence for his position: *For, as Holy Scripture saith: "Of Him, and through Him, and to Him, are all things: to whom be glory for ever. Amen." And hence all things must desire and yearn for and must love the Beautiful and the Good.*[57]

This quote-within-a-quote tips us off to the thin disguise worn by this late fifth-century author. Comprised of ten brief letters and four major treatises, they are all addressed to various persons of the first-century church. The longest works, the four treatises, are addressed to Timothy, who is supposedly the famous biblical character by that name who traveled with Paul. The letters are addressed to other well-known first-century personages, including the Apostle John.

However, a first-century Christian would hardly quote from the works of a contemporary like Paul and call it "Holy Scripture." Paul's letters were not considered scriptural until much later. The only "Holy Scripture" first-century Christians had was the Greek translation of the Hebrew Bible. In fact, a large part of the Jewish Bible was not considered scriptural until the rabbinic conference at Jamnia closed the canon of the "Old"

Testament forever. That conference met in A.D. 90, almost thirty years after Paul's death.

Even though Dionysius wrote under a pen name, his insights are immeasurably influential on medieval and later reformational mysticism. His quote from Paul's letter to the Romans shows us that by the fifth century people were reinterpreting the early writings of the faith to see their true mystical content. His use of this passage shows that Dionysius correctly saw an early Christian doxology in Paul's works which pointed toward the doctrine of one Power and one Presence. A natural outgrowth of this insight is to see that if God is all-present and all-powerful, that which we call evil can have no permanence. Dionysius went beyond this idea to affirm, with modern metaphysical Christians and neo-Platonists throughout history, that evil is less than temporary: it has no real existence at all.

2. *Nonexistence of Evil.* If God is "the Beautiful and Good" from which everything "exists and comes into being," a logical conclusion can be drawn that evil cannot come from God. And since everything comes from God, evil cannot truly be said to exist. It is

shadow, not substance. Dionysius writes: *For even as fire cannot cool us, so Good cannot produce the things which are not good. And if all things that have been come from the Good . . . then nothing in the world cometh of evil. Then evil cannot even in any wise exist . . .* [58]

A problem with this line of thought has always been that human beings perceive evil in the world around them. Philosopher Jean-Paul Sartre and existentialist author Albert Camus were two French intellectuals who denied any value system which pointed to objective evil. Yet, when the Nazi war machine invaded their land and they experienced the tyranny of Hitler's scheme to create a "master race," French intellectuals like these two great men joined the resistance and fought the evil. How can there be no evil when we encounter it in the world around us?

Dionysius is no ivory-tower optimist. He acknowledges that people can choose to do terrible things to their fellow human beings, things we see as very definite evils. His answer is that evil is the lack of good, just as dark is lack of light. When someone puts out a lamp, darkness occurs. However, only light exists as a force, not darkness which is its absence. It makes no sense to sit in the dark denying that dark happens, Dionysius would say. However, we have no way of generating dark. Dark can only come about when light is removed, just as cold can only exist when heat is not present.

Dionysius never owned a refrigerator, but he would have understood immediately the principles of refrigeration: remove heat. Our air conditioners and freezers never create cold, they remove heat. The result is a lesser heat which we call cold. Although a fifth-century thinker like Dionysius could not have known it, there is a point (-273 degrees centigrade) which marks the lowest possible temperature. Nothing can get colder than absolute zero, because at -273 degrees centigrade there is no heat whatsoever. So the cold we feel is really best understood as varying degrees of warmth. Heat alone has reality; cold is its absence.

As with light and heat, so goes good in opposition to evil. Evil has no power or reality; it is the absence of good. Dionysius believed that there are degrees in human character, too. Some souls are at a lower state of spirituality than others and so reflect less divine Light. We might call these persons "evil," when in reality they represent a lesser degree of good. Dionysius says: *Some creatures participate wholly in the Good, others are lacking in It less or more, and others possess a still fainter participation therein, while to others the Good is present as but the faintest echo.*[59]

This is due not to their nature but to their choices, Dionysius contended, since their natures are derived from God and are therefore Good. But what about the demons mentioned in Scripture? Surely they must be evil! Not so, wrote Dionysius. He boldly delivered this blow to orthodox demonology: *Nor are the devils naturally evil. For, were they such, they would not have sprung from the Good ... how can the devils be evil since they sprung from God? For the Good produceth and createth good things ... they are not evil by their natural constitution not only through a lack of angelic virtues.*[60]

Dionysius was a bold thinker who was not afraid of controversy, although we can understand his desire for anonymity when we read passages like this. His method of achieving spiritual illumination likewise employed an unconventional, mystical route, the *via negativa* or "way of negation." There are hints of

Eastern theology in Dionysius, especially in his highly developed doctrine about the nature of God, which that early mystic approached via negation.

3. *Impersonal Nature of God: Via Negativa.* According to Dionysius, the supreme goal of life is to become one with God. This, he counseled, could be achieved only through mystical meditation and prayer. However, he also believed in illumination as a tool to enhance mystical experiences. Dionysius, and through him many great thinkers afterward, taught that we can best understand God by meditating on what He is not. He writes to Timothy, advising him: *Do thou, dear Timothy, in thy eager striving ... abandon both sense-perception and mental activity ... and as far as possible mount up with knowledge into union with the One who is above all being and knowledge; for by freeing thyself completely and unconditionally from thyself and from all things, thou shalt come to the superessential brightness of the divine darkness ....* [61]

Dionysius believed that we can say only what God is not; He is not limited, not restrained, not personal. Yet, we can say that He is good, because He is beyond goodness.

We can say that He is love, because He is beyond loving-kindness. All our statements about God must be affirmed and denied at the same time, because He is far beyond our meager efforts to conceive of Him. Thus everything we say about God is symbolic.

4. *Symbolic Theology.* Dionysius provides a theological base for people like Paul Tillich, one of the twentieth century's great theologians, when he writes that all our ideas of God are symbolic in nature. Any God we can conceptualize in our limited way must necessarily be wrong. Therefore, any symbol we invent to talk about God—Omnipotence, Omnipresence—must be affirmed and denied at the same time. Christian symbols like the Cross can reveal the nature of God's saving love. But every symbol has in it the danger of becoming the reality it tries to symbolize: the Cross becomes Christianity, the Bible becomes the Word of God and perhaps even God Himself. We must symbolize, because we cannot conceive of the true greatness of God. We cannot even understand the complexities of a single place, like a major city, let alone the Creator of all the universe. Therefore, all our God-talk is symbolic in nature.

Dionysius influenced many thinkers who would come later. Thomas Aquinas, Meister Eckehart, and all the mystics after him would owe him a great debt. There are passages in Dionysius that suggest he was read by some of the founding fathers of Unity, too. Look at the amazing similarity between his work and a passage from H. Emilie Cady's *Lessons in Truth:*

Dionysius: *For as our sun, through no choice or deliberation, but by the very fact of its existence, gives light to all those things which have any inherent power of sharing its illumination, even so God sends forth upon all things according to their receptive powers, the rays of Its undivided Goodness.*[62]

Cady: *We do not have to beseech God any more than we have to beseech the sun to shine. The sun shines because it is a law of its being to shine, and it cannot help it. No more can God help pouring into us unlimited wisdom, power, all good, because to give is a law of His being.*[63]

One Power/One Presence, the nonexistence of evil as a force, the impersonal nature of God, symbolic theology. Dionysius anticipated the main thrust of modern mystical/ metaphysical theology more than 1500 years ago. But his work did not just collect dust on the shelves of monasteries. In the darkest hour of the Dark Ages another hero of the faith read the good news of God's one Power and Presence and then set to work developing these ideas to an even deeper understanding of the divine plan. It is to this lonely beacon in the night season of church history we shall now turn our attention.

5

Philosopher of Spiritual Evolution/Involution John Scotus Erigena (9th Century A.D.)

Dionysius the Areopagite wrote in Koine Greek, the common tongue of business and commerce in the late classical world. Because Alexander the Great left centers of learning and culture around the world in his wake, Koine became the *lingua franca* of Western civilization. Thus our New Testament was written not in Hebrew (which by the time of Jesus was already a dead language) nor Aramaic (which the early followers and disciples probably spoke), but in Koine, the language of international communication. Even Caesar's Roman officials spoke Greek; the official business of the Empire was conducted in Koine.

However, with respectability and power, the Roman Church began to shift its internal correspondence from bothersome other-language formality to a simpler version of Latin, the Vulgate or vernacular Latin. Jerome, mentioned in an earlier study on Pelagius, translated the Bible into Latin Vulgate as early as the fifth century. Since reading in any language was a highly special-ized skill (comparable to today's computer programmers who design whole systems), there were very few people outside the Church who mastered the written word in their own language, let alone gained any facil-ity in a foreign tongue.

Because it was the common language of the early medieval church, Latin slowly but sure-ly nudged Koine Greek out of the picture. Ironically, Latin refused to give up center stage once it had the limelight. As the lan-guages of Western civilization continued to evolve, Latin, like Hebrew, Aramaic, and Koine, became a dead language. But its hold on church theology and policy was so firm that Christian clergy in the Catholic Church continued to communicate in it until the twentieth century. Jerome's Vulgate Bible and the Latin Mass clung tenaciously to its unchallenged position as repositories of Truth for fifteen centuries, long after the last Latin-speaking native linguist had made his transition beyond this life.

So Latin, introduced to bring commonly spoken language to the church's worship and Scriptures, eventually became the greatest hindrance to popular understanding in the largest body of Christians. By the time of our next ancestor in the ancient faith, the ninth century, Latin was already a scholarly and priestly language quite distant from the illiterate masses who could not even read their own languages. And this inability to read was not restricted to peasants. Kings, nobles, and virtually all women remained illiterate. Reading was a specialized skill, the exclusive province of the clergy. When the Bible was read, it was read by a clergyperson who gave the church's interpretation of what the text meant. As Latin died out, the biblical witness became ever further removed from the people: not only was it written, it was written in a dead language. The hold of the clergy on exclusive rights to interpret Truth was complete.

After the fall of Rome, world culture did an interesting flip-flop. Instead of the center of the former Empire, the very fringe of Roman civilization became the bank where learning was kept on deposit. Roman legions never conquered Scotland or Ireland, but Christian missionaries brought the fiercely independent Celts into the mainstream of civilization by converting them to the ancient faith. With typical zeal, the Irish embraced Christianity and set about establishing centers of study on the far northwest coast of their island nation.

It was these monasteries on the seaward side of Ireland, the farthest edge of European civilization, which delivered Western culture from its dark night of the soul, the cultural anarchy following the fall of Rome. Many of the writings from ancient civilization that are extant today come from copies laboriously penned by Irish monks sitting at their desks fighting sleep and shivering from cold winds blowing in off the North Atlantic.

Historian Paul Johnson remarks that the scholars of the Dark Ages labored in the shadow of greater darkness to come: *There was a sense of gloomy urgency about the task, for men believed that, however horrible*

the period since Rome's decline had been,
things would get worse, not better . . . .[64]

In the ninth century, King Alfred insisted
that his scholars press on with translation of
the essential Latin texts into Old English
because he firmly believed the time was fast
approaching when no one would any longer
be able to read Latin.[65] It was in this gathering intellectual long winter's night that one
of the bright stars in the history of Christian
thought rose over the Irish horizon.

His name was John, but in the medieval
period middle names and surnames were not
usually handed down within families. Celebrated personages often became known by
accomplishments or attributes, not always
complimentary ones at that. Thus we have
William the Conqueror and Ethelred the
Unready, Charles the Great (Charlemagne)
and Peter the Hermit. By far the most common last names given by history to great
figures of the past are related to geography:
Francis of Assisi, Joan of Arc, Catherine of
Siena, and so on. John came from Ireland
(*Scotus* in Latin), so he became known as
John the Irishman born in Erin or *Johannes*
Scotus Erigena.

In his multivolume work, "The Story of

Civilization," Will Durant says that Erigena, although not a clergyman nor a monk, was a man of vast learning, quite competent in Greek and knowledgeable in the classics. Durant also reports that John was "something of a wit." Durant writes: *Charles the Bald, dining with him asked him, "What distinguishes* (literally, "what separates") *a fool from an Irishman?" to which John is said to have answered, "The table."*[66]

Erigena must have been educated in Irish schools related to the monasteries in some way, for he displays an extraordinary knowledge of theology and church doctrine as well as Greek. He was born around the year 810 and moved to France in the 840s where he became the in-house scholar and theologian for King Charles. Despite Erigena's counter barb, or perhaps because of it, Charles the Bald liked John and protected him when the theologian ran into trouble with church authorities over doctrinal arguments. In this relationship between a secular ruler and a radical religious thinker, we see anticipation of the similar bond which will exist in the sixteenth century between the Elector Frederick the Wise and his famous radical thinker Martin Luther. Both John in the ninth century and Luther in the sixteenth had the good fortune and good sense to win support from people who held the reins of power in their immediate vicinity. Without this relationship, both would have been just two more heretics burned at the stake. This suggests that, despite the idealism which characterizes John's writings, he knew the secular world has its own "golden rule": the people with the gold make the rules. Less realistic reformers have not lasted long enough to make such an impact as Luther or even as Erigena, as we shall see.

John got into trouble the first time during a debate over the sacraments, but his writings on this subject have not survived. We know that Erigena's opponents cried that he did not believe in the "real presence" of Christ's body and blood in the eucharistic meal, seeing them as symbolic rather than literal. More than this we do not know.

The next controversy John entered into is fully documented, however. A German monk named Gottschalk was preaching absolute predestinarianism, thereby denying that men and women have free will. Predestination has been debated in the Christian church since the early days. Augustine held this view, as did the great Protestant reformer John Calvin. *Calvinism*, in fact, is almost a theological synonym for predestinarianism. However, the mainline of Christian thought has usually leaned toward human freedom and away from predestination. The Middle Ages saw a high degree of interest in predestination, perhaps more people held this view in medieval times than in any other time before or since.

Archbishop Hincmar saw Gottschalk's preaching as dangerous. As Pelagius had pointed out in his debate with Augustine, if we do not believe man has free will, we relieve him of the responsibility to make ethical and moral decisions. A believer in absolute predestination can comfortably ignore poverty, war, racism, and nuclear proliferation. If all of this was determined long ago and we have no free moral agency, all human effort is equally pointless. Thus in a very paradoxical way those who believe in total predestination are actually in league with those who believe in no God at all, for both see human values operating fruitlessly: the atheist says there are no moral standards, and the predestinarian says we have no power to act, morally or otherwise.

Erigena's reputation as a scholar and controversialist earned him an invitation from Hincmar to write a refutation of Gottschalk. John accepted, gleefully cutting a swath through not only Gottschalk's predestination, but the whole concept of any restraint on the exercise of human freedom and human reason. He charged Gottschalk with heresy and ignorance, for John contended that God not only allows people the right to choose evil but really doesn't know what they are going to choose, either. If God knew evil, He would be the cause of it, Erigena declared.

Most profound, however, was his attack on the principle of church authority and tradition. John was a Christian philosopher in an age when philosophy was suspect. In the medieval period one did not speculate or use new arguments to discover Truth. The pattern was to find an ancient authority and quote it, preferably, an ancient orthodox church father. Scientific investigation and experimentation, such as we take for granted today, was simply not part of the mental equipment.

Thus the Church could call before its Inquisition an aging Galileo and force him to recant his heretical notion that the Earth revolves around the sun. Although he had looked through his telescope and seen the universe firsthand, such evidence was not admissible because it conflicted with the ancient authorities.

There is even a story, perhaps apocryphal, of a church council which fell to debating how many legs the common housefly owned. Various authorities were cited, but the conference was getting nowhere. Finally an exasperated young cleric stood and suggested they catch a fly and count the legs. He was rudely expelled from the meeting, and the council subsequently declared that it was a mystery of God and no one would ever know the answer.

Such thinking is so totally alien to our thought processes that we find it incredible. Yet, ancient authorities were the sole basis for consideration of Truth during medieval times. John Scotus Erigena would have none of this. In his attack on Gottschalk, John boldly began with an uncompromising word of praise for philosophical speculation: *In earnestly investigating and attempting to discover the reason of all things, every means of attaining to a pious and perfect doctrine lies in that science and discipline which the Greeks call philosophy.*[67]

Durant comments that Erigena's refutation was more heretical than Gottschalk's sermons. Councils in 855 and 859 condemned both of them. Gottschalk remained a prisoner at his monastery until his death; but John's patron, Charles, protected the uncompromising Irishman.

Other currents of history were moving to bring into John's hands the work of another of our friends, Dionysius the Areopagite, whom we met in the previous study. By this time, Christendom had split into two major subdivisions, East and West. The Eastern Church was known as the Byzantine because its capital, Constantinople, was built at the site of a village previously known as Byzantium. The Eastern Church still spoke Greek, since its greatest population was ethnically Greek.

In 824 the Byzantine Emperor Michael the Stammerer sent a copy of Dionysius' works to the Western Church. However, since it was in Koine Greek, no one could read it even at the highest levels of church and state. No one, that is, but a great scholar educated in Ireland, John Scotus Erigena. Although they doubted his orthodoxy, they never questioned his ability. He got the manuscript and

proceeded to translate the wildly mystical
writings of Pseudo-Dionysius into medieval
Latin. Of course, at this time everyone believed the works were genuine products of the
apostolic age, so they carried special status in
a world dominated by appeals to ancient
authority.

John fell in love with these works, culling
from their pages ideas like the nonexistence
of evil, metaphysical/allegorical interpretation of the Bible, and other neo-Platonic concepts which the Eastern Church with its more
mystical approach to theology had long
favored. The West, following the lead of Tertullian and Augustine, became legalistic.
Salvation was put in terms of obedience to
Church and God, in that order. In the
Eastern Church, the long-standing tradition
had been to see Christianity as a mystical
religion through which believers became
united with God in Christ.

Sitting alone in his study, John Scotus
Erigena discovered this difference in the
writings of Dionysius. From that time forward, John was freed from legalism and
ready to explore intellectually the idea
that there is only one Power and Presence,
God, the good omnipotent. He abandoned

whatever shreds of legalism his mind had
clung to and took off on a speculative flight
unprecedented in the history of world religious thinking. Arthur Cushman McGiffert
summarizes Erigena's theological position in
"A History of Christian Thought," Volume
II: *The divine nature embraces everything;
apart from God or outside of him there is
nothing. He is Being unlimited and undiffer-
entiated; the world is Being circumscribed
and divided. The unity between God and the
creature is complete; he is in all things and is
the being of all. When we say that God
created everything, we mean that he is in
everything as its essence, the common substance of all that is ... Spirits and bodies, all
things that exist are but manifestations of
him; each is a genuine theophany.*[68]

Moreover, God is not only everywhere-
present for Erigena, God and man are so held
in unity that they are not really two but one
and the same.[69] John made great use of the
Bible but was in no way hampered by it. He
assumed it was to be read metaphysically/
allegorically. Erigena writes: *Do not be
alarmed, for now we must follow reason
which investigates the truth of things, and
overpowered by no authority and in no way*

*shackled, sets forth and proclaims openly
what it has studiously examined and laboriously discovered.*[70]

If there were medals given for heroism
retroactive to the ninth century, perhaps
John the Irishman should receive the Medal
of Honor. The courage it took to stand alone
at the height of the Dark Ages and proclaim
Truth as he saw it—regardless of the re-
sponse of authority—cannot be fully grasped
by us, who live in a free society. People were
broken on the rack for much less. Yet, John
continued to teach Truth fearlessly, though
council after council and Pope after Pope
ruled his works heretical. He responded to
the anathemas from churchly authority with
characteristic coolness: *Authority sometimes
proceeds from reason, but reason never from
authority. For all authority that is not
approved by true reason seems weak. But
true reason, since it rests on its own strength,
needs no reinforcement.*[71]

Will Durant observed: *Here is the Age of
Reason moving in the womb of the Age of
Faith.*[72] It would take many centuries before
Christianity could become practical, draw-
ing its beliefs again from the core of bibli-
cal teachings and demonstrating them in

everyday life. Appeal to authority would continue unabated until the revolutionary thinking of people like George Fox, William Ellery Channing, Emerson, and Theodore Parker. We shall discuss the contributions of these men in subsequent studies.

Thus unfettered by the limitations of official doctrine, Erigena's mind sailed like Jonathan Livingston Seagull, flying away from and above the flock, discovering the way living was meant to be. We cannot leave his thought until we examine his central thesis, an idea which would wait eleven centuries until other great thinkers like Charles Fillmore and Teilhard de Chardin spoke their truths. As early as the mid-ninth century, John Scotus Erigena was talking about cosmic evolution/involution.

Four Stages of Divine Evolution/Involution

1) *God.* God as the Uncreated, Eternal— this is where John begins his system. Just as astrophysics tells us that over fifteen billion years ago there was an aggregation of all matter in a great mass which exploded outward (the Big Bang theory), theological writers like Erigena and much later Teilhard

de Chardin see all existence issuing from God. In essence, John taught that God created everything out of Himself—He flung bits of Himself to the far corners of the universe where they are to grow back to awareness of their oneness with God. For Erigena, this happens in stages. Stage one, God, sends forth divine ideas, stage two.

2) *Divine ideas.* These are the models from which everything is created. God's creative power moves from pure energy to organization of reality. We might use a modern analogy and see this as God's game plan for all time. Everything which exists then comes forth from these divine ideas. In this John echoes the Gospel of John when it proclaims that through the Logos (Divine Mind) everything was created.

3) *World of Sensation.* We and all created things are part of the sensible world, the physical world. Matter is not eternal for Erigena, but came into being as the divine ideas worked their game plan. Matter is real, but not everlasting. All things and all beings are really God-power manifested in different form. As time passes, all will be once again taken back up into God.

4) *Consummation.* Chardin calls this the

Omega Point; we would call it Christ-consciousness. Thus God sends forth His own energy, creates divine ideas, through them creates things, gives us free will so that we can choose to find our way back to Him once more. For John Scotus Erigena, Jesus Christ is absolutely essential to this process, because in Jesus we have an open door to our own Christ-consciousness. Through faith in Jesus, we are quite literally new creations.

Not all modern Truth students would agree with everything he taught, but we can certainly marvel that such ideas were possible a thousand years before Darwin popularized the notion of organic evolution and metaphysical Christianity pointed toward a parallel spiritual development. Yet, this is precisely the point of all our investigations— New Thought is not new. Glimmers of these ideas have reappeared again and again in the history of Christianity. Often opposed by orthodox authority, such imaginative interpretations of the Christian witness have surfaced other places in the thinking and prayer life of these underground saints.

It is not mere speculation which makes a person like John Scotus Erigena a great church father of metaphysical Christianity—

speculation can be a lazy man's excuse not to do his theological homework. Rather, because Erigena stood within the Church and doggedly refused to let the orthodox define the terms for him, he deserves our applause and thanks. In his own words, he describes his life goal, an ambition we might all do well to emulate: *True authority does not oppose right reason, nor right reason true authority. For it is not to be doubted that both come from one source, namely, the divine wisdom.*[73]

John Scotus Erigena—Christian philosopher, speculative genius, heroic and unorthodox churchman—another of our ancestors who nudged humanity along its path toward better understandings of the Divine. His mystical/metaphysical insights can still inspire us almost 1200 years after he wrote and lived.

We now turn to the last representative of the medieval church whom we shall study in this survey of mystical/metaphysical backgrounds. The high mysticism of the Middle Ages would find no greater expression than in the sermons and writings of a Dominican priest who joyfully proclaimed the divinity of humanity to his bewildered congregation of cloistered nuns. Such a consistent factor was he that no text could be written about medieval theology which failed to mention this unorthodox preacher. His beliefs almost cost him his life. But his tenacity in the face of danger has immeasurably enhanced the body of Christian mystical writings. We turn next to Meister Eckehart.

6

The Spark of the Soul
Meister Eckehart
(1260-1327)

There is something powerful, deep, and moving about the works of the Dominican friar named Eckehart whom history has dubbed with the continuing title of "Meister" (master).

Eckehart was a thinker with a world-embracing vision and a zeal for God. He was one of those God-intoxicated souls like the great Hasidic Rabbis, or Catholic mystics like Catherine of Siena, or Protestant lovers of God like the Wesleys (founders of Methodism). He wrote intellectually, but sometimes divine love overflowed and he threw aside logic to proclaim his joy in the Lord. *Up noble Soul,* he wrote, *put on thy dancing shoes!*

Eckehart wrote in Latin and German, but neither language could adequately express the vastness of his view of the divine panorama. Here are a few brief examples: *When I think about the kingdom of God, I am struck dumb by its grandeur; for the kingdom of God is God Himself with all his fullness . . . all the worlds one could imagine God creating would still not be as the kingdom of God . . . . Nobody ever wanted anything as much as God wants to bring people to know him. God is always ready but we are not ready. God is near to us but we are far from him. God is within; we are without. God is at home; we are abroad.*[74]

And this passage about God's love for us: *Now, you must know that God loves the soul so strenuously that to take this privilege of loving from God would be to take his life and being. It would be to kill God, if one may use such an expression. For out of God's love for the soul, the Holy Spirit blooms and the Holy Spirit is that love. Since, then, the soul is so strenuously loved by God, it must be of great importance . . . .*[75]

Eckehart had a ring to his writing style that later echoed in the style of Charles Fillmore. He, like Fillmore, was not afraid to follow a line of thought wherever it took him, because he was rooted firmly in divine truth and held love for God above all else.

More importantly for students of metaphysical Christianity, Eckehart's mysticism sprang from the belief that saw the Good as omnipotent, all-pervasive. And he was not hesitant to dip into non-Christian sources to cite others who shared his viewpoints. He quotes the greatest medieval rabbi, perhaps the greatest Jewish scholar of all time, Moses Maimonides. And during a time of hostility between Moslems and Christians, Eckehart showed his universalism by reading and quoting from the brilliant medieval Islamic philosophers Averroes and Avicenna. In pursuit of truth, it never occurred to Eckehart that there were any racial, religious, or ethnic barriers worthy of respect. God was his objective; he would not be slowed down by anything or anyone in his "dance" of up-reaching love.

We know very little of Eckehart's early life. He was born Johannes Eckehart, probably in the year 1260. In those days, births were seldom recorded unless the child was heir to a title or property holdings. "John" Eckehart had neither. However, he did have a keen intellect and was soon enrolled as a novice in the convent of Dominican Friars at Erfurt, Germany.

For many centuries, children of low birth had very few avenues for upward mobility. Bound to the land as serfs under the feudal system, they were virtual slaves to the lord of their local town or country estate (manor). They were not permitted an education, nor were they allowed to join the military service except as pack carriers and work crews. These carried no more benefits than landed serfdom, so most peasants dreaded the frequent wars that swept through their lands taking lives and crops from their poor villages.

Yet there was one avenue of escape for children of exceptional promise: the Church. In the Middle Ages the Church stood as guardian of learning, the sole place where a young person of ability and ambition could rise on his or her merit to a position of some respectability and power. It cost the youth his or her right to marry and have relationships with members of the opposite sex, not to mention the grueling pace of monastic life. But in the world of the serf, this was a price worth paying.

This was the course chosen by Johannes Eckehart. A bright lad, he was wise enough to choose the Dominican order and thus ensure development of his preaching skills as well as a good chance for further education and university professorships. Various religious orders took on special functions as the structure of medieval Christianity evolved. The Dominicans became known as the Preaching Order because public speaking was their speciality.

As the university system—borrowed from the Arabs—grew, departments established teaching posts which to this day are called "chairs." There was a chair of history, a chair of theology, a chair of biblical studies, and so on. These chairs were the exclusive property of religious orders, so the Dominicans jealously guarded their teaching posts and ensured that their people filled the chairs. Other orders which did not have access to these positions were always trying to get a man into a chair so that they could have a precedent established for the future. Thus, orders with teaching chairs were careful whom they sent to the post, since they prized these jobs so highly.

Eckehart was chosen not only to go on in his studies to the Universty of Paris, but was eventually given lectureships and held a chair. This means young Eckehart was an outstanding churchman, far above his peers. No one of less ability would obtain such a post, lest he fail at the job and be replaced by someone of another order.

Eckehart taught at the University of Paris, held various important administrative positions in his order, and generally displayed good rapport within his brotherhood and the Church at large. In fact, he might never have caused controversy had it not been for another aspect of his role as a Dominican: his preaching in the German vernacular.

Meister Eckehart made no attempt to conceal his mysticism. He preached it in the common language of the people from pulpit after pulpit. Often his congregations were comprised of nuns who were under his spiritual guidance. His sermons must have flown high over the heads of these folks, but his popularity was enormous.

To understand Eckehart we must understand Scholasticism, the new philosophy of the high Middle Ages championed by his predecessor in Paris, Thomas Aquinas. It would be Eckehart's contribution to Christianity to take the intellectual concepts of Scholasticism and give them expression through prayer, mystical practices, and preaching. Paul Tillich describes his role: *They (the medieval mystics) were not speculative monks sitting alongside of the world, but they wanted people to have the possibility of experiencing what was expressed in the scholastic systems. Thus the mysticism of Eckehart unites the most abstract scholastic concepts—especially that of being—with a burning soul, with the warmth of religious feeling and the love-power of religious acting.*[76]

Since Meister Eckehart was a Dominican and a mystic, it was natural that he should employ mysticism in service of the great concepts annunciated by the paramount religious scholar of medieval times, Thomas Aquinas. Where Thomas had been a thinker, Eckehart was a preacher and a doer. The Meister wanted humans to experience God, not just read about Him. The influence of *Thomism* (or the philosophy of Thomas Aquinas) prevails to this day, but when

Eckehart began his ministry, Aquinas had just died. In fact, the two men were contemporaries and might have known each other if Thomas had not died in 1275 at age fifty.

It remained for the greatest Dominican mystic, Meister Eckehart, to make practical and apply the ideas of the greatest Dominican scholar, the "angelic Doctor" as he was known, St. Thomas Aquinas. For us to understand one we must grasp the teachings of the other.

To comprehend the Scholasticism of medieval times, we must go back in time to ancient Greece and examine the contrasting philosophies of two other contemporaries, Plato and Aristotle. As students of world history know, Socrates taught Plato; Plato taught Aristotle; and Aristotle taught Alexander the Great, who tried to teach it to the world. That is why Greek culture spread so widely and the Greek language became the *lingua franca* of the educated ancient world.

One would think that with all this chain of command in educational matters, the philosophies of Plato and Aristotle would be highly compatible. Nothing could be further from the truth, for Aristotle repudiated the central thesis of his master's worldview and substituted a radically opposite view of reality.

Plato had held that true reality is in an unseen ideal world, the world of divine ideas. He taught that human beings were capable of directly contacting this unseen realm and gaining personal insights into ultimate reality. In fact, a true Platonist might even doubt that matter has any reality. Only in the realm of divine ideas do we find real Truth.

Aristotle insisted, on the other hand, that all human knowledge comes through the senses and is the result of direct or indirect sensory input. If you believe in a realm of unseen ideas, Aristotle would assert, it is because you heard or read that concept through your senses of hearing or sight. Only experiences in the world give us knowledge, for Aristotelians.[77]

Historian Arthur Cushman McGiffert writes of this conflict: *Nothing could well be more opposed than these two views. They represent indeed two radically different philosophical tendencies. It is evident at a glance that such a theory of knowledge such as Aristotle's was out of line with traditional Christian ideas. How on such a supposition could the Christian claim to know God and come into communion with him?*[78]

Churchmen violently opposed Aristotelianism when it began seeping into Christendom through Muslim Spain. The great Arab scholars saved much of the ancient world's philosophy and literature for modern humanity to wrestle with and enjoy. However, this new burst of Aristotelianism caused quite a flurry in medieval Europe. McGiffert compares the resistance to Aristotle with the great outcry of many churchmen over the new theories of Charles Darwin at the end of the nineteenth century. Most intelligent Christians realized quickly that evolution was an idea whose time had come and could not be ignored without great peril to the cause of truth. The great majority of Christian scholars today accept evolution and no longer see it as a force opposed to biblical Truth, even though the opponents of evolution tend to be a vocal minority clamoring to be heard.

Likewise, Thomas Aquinas and those who came after him in the scholastic tradition realized that Aristotle was a force to be reckoned with, not shouted down nor ignored. Thomas set to work reinterpreting the traditional doctrines of the Christian faith in the light of those truths which Aristotelian logic gave him.

McGiffert says: *In spite of the difficulties Thomas combined Aristotelianism and Christian theology and he did it by drawing two sharp distinctions: the one between natural and revealed theology and the other between the condition of knowledge in this life and in the next.*[79]

Aquinas held that both Plato and Aristotle were right—there is an unseen realm which contains divine ideas, and yet we know things of this world only through our senses. The belief that we learn about God through our power of reason was from Aristotle. This is a kind of reaching upward toward heaven. But we learn about God more perfectly through His revelation to us, especially His revelation to us in Jesus Christ, this is modified Platonism. So we have natural theology (Aristotelian reaching upward) and revealed religion (Platonic divine ideas known directly to us in Jesus Christ).[80]

Meister Eckehart took this raw scholastic data and produced a remarkable life of faith based on its central teachings. But where Thomas insisted that full knowledge of God was possible in the Platonic sense only in the world to come, Eckehart claimed that we could have it here. Not full knowledge of God in His completeness, but a glimmer of that completeness. He called the place where God is known to an individual person the *Seelenfünklein* or "spark of the soul."[81] It was a highly controversial theology in his day and provoked outrage from conservative Church leaders.

Eckehart believed that man could know God three ways, although only one of them was a sure kind of knowledge: sensibly, rationally, and super-rationally. We can see in the world the hand mark of God's presence. We can logically infer that there must be a Source of goodness and beauty. However, only when we abandon sensory pursuits and rational inquiry, only when we mount up on wings of praise and ecstacy, can we come to an awareness of God's reality.

If we commune with God, love and live for Him, questions about His existence seem equally absurd. This is the essence of what Eckehart said. And he went beyond this to even more intimate terms about our relationship to God.

God can be known to us because God and we are one. This union is not just a harmony of wills or a spiritual communion; Eckehart envisions complete fusion of the individual with God like a drop of water returning to the sea.

Eckehart preached this idea in a sermon on "Renewal in the Spirit." He told his congregation: *God must become I, and I must become God.... The fire changes into itself whatever is brought to it, and gives it its own nature. The wood does not change the fire into wood; rather the fire changes wood into fire. Thus we are transformed into God and know him as he is....*[82]

Eckehart believed God and man could be united because they were already one. It is not that we are simply made in the image and likeness of God; we share in the very nature of God. We are truly divine beings, offspring of God the Father.

For Eckehart, the key is consciousness. He preached: *If the wood knew about God and were conscious how near he is, as the highest angel is conscious of it, the wood would have the same blessedness as the angel.*[83]

What about human consciousness? Eckehart assured his flock that we partake of greater blessings because we have greater awareness of our divine nature: *Therefore man is more blessed than a stick of wood, because he recognizes God and knows how near God is. The more conscious of it the more blessed, the less conscious of it the less blessed he is. He is not blessed because God is in him and near to him, or because he has God, but only because he is aware of God . . . .*[84]

Eckehart and other mystics in Christian tradition believed direct communion between the individual worshiper and God was possible. What separated him and those he influenced from other mystics was this proclamation of the oneness of God and man. He has often been accused of *pantheism,* the belief that everything is God—the tree, the stone, man. Pantheism reduces God to the sum total of all things; God is the universe. Eckehart would not agree, because his concept of God far transcended the mere physical universe.

In fact, the Meister had a concept of divinity so lofty that he acknowledged the futility of all concepts to express the inexpressible depth of God. *If you can understand anything about him,* he writes, *it in no way belongs to him.*[85] Any God-concept we could comprehend would necessarily be wrong, falling far short of the true grandeur of divinity which God alone perceives about Himself.

In places Eckehart's writings are virtual poetry. He coaxes his parishioners to turn wholly to God and enter the silence of His presence through prayer and meditation. He even taught centering prayer—using that term—like Unity practices in its guided meditations during worship. And how does a soul ascend unto divinity? Eckehart believed the essence of spiritual growth could be summed up in one word—*detachment*. He writes: *True detachment means a mind as little moved by what befalls, by joy and sorrow, honor and disgrace, as a broad mountain by a gentle breeze.*[86]

Why detachment? Because God is free from all worries and problems; God is the Infinite and lacks nothing. Since He lacks nothing, He needs nothing. He is motionless, still, silent, beyond thought and action, beyond all possible concepts. Only in the *Seelenfünklein*, the spark of the soul where God touches our finite minds with a hint of divinity, does God appear to us, and then only as a feeling which translates as absurdity when one tries to describe such an experience.

In all this we hear continually the echoing

voices of Philo, Origen, Dionysius, and Erigena, as well as hints of those we shall yet discuss: Fox, Emerson, Tillich, and Chardin. McGiffert says that Eckehart reminds him of Dionysius, and especially of Erigena. The historian writes: *Whether Eckehart drew directly upon that great thinker (Erigena) . . . at any rate his (Eckehart's) thought moved along similar lines. Not altogether inappropriately he might be called a mystical Erigena or Erigena become mystic.*[87]

Eckehart was attacked by more conservative churchmen, as prophets tend to be. His works were condemned in a Papal bull known as "In Agro Dominico" which translates from the Latin as "In the Field of the Lord," the phrase with which the bull (decree) begins. Note that the Latin wording is perhaps a play on the word *Dominican,* reflecting power politics within the Church at large between Eckehart's Dominican order and other groups. The bull was published after a series of charges had been leveled against him by church officials.

Eckehart replied to the charges, denying any of them were true and heaping abuse upon those who attacked him. The tactic was not effective, for the charges stood. He died before the bull was made public, thus was spared any possible punishment for his crimes of heresy.

His legacy to modern mystical Christianity is profound. He saw the world, like Erigena before him, as part of an eternal process of evolution/involution, unfolding and refolding, growth and change. He believed the scholastics were right, that there is evidence for God in the physical world and in the realm of ideas. He took these abstract concepts and put them into practice. In this respect, he might be called the first father of practical Christianity.

Always reaching for the unattainable, Eckehart had the courage to say from the pulpit that God and man are a Unity. He told the German nuns—no doubt to their astonishment if they followed his argument at all—that he and the Father were One: *The eye wherewith I see God is the same eye wherewith God sees me. My eye and God's eye are one eye—one seeing, one knowing, one loving . . . I say more: he begets me not alone as his Son, he begets me as himself and himself as me—me his essence and his nature.*[88]

With the ecstatic words of Meister Eckehart ringing through the ages, we leave those marvelous medieval mystics and move to the next major group of forerunners to Unity. In the works of George Fox, Georg Hegel, Ralph Waldo Emerson, and his disciple Theodore Parker, we find all the spiritual, intellectual, and systematic foundations on which nineteenth-century metaphysicians will construct modern New Thought Christianity. So we shall call this period—from the late days of the radical reformation of the seventeenth century through the Enlightenment to the Unitarian Controversy of the nineteenth century—"Setting the Stage." It will prove a good description, as you will see. We begin with the first Quaker.

Part III

Setting the Stage

7

The Cheerful Walker
George Fox
(1624-1691)

How do you describe a man like George Fox? In any age he would be considered extraordinary. Unlettered, he challenged and triumphed over learned adversaries. Untitled, he took on the power of the established Church of England which was backed by the King. Uncultured, he attracted followers from the humblest to the highest levels of society. Unordained, he founded a religious movement which spanned two continents and has wielded tremendous influence on Western civilization. Unafraid, he stood before judges and rulers who had the power to imprison, physically chastise, and even kill him for his religious views.

Through it all, he managed to maintain a positive, healthy attitude and a firm belief that Truth would prevail. He told the ministers and missionaries who went forth teaching his vision of a Christianity restored that they were to *walk cheerfully over the earth, answering that of God in everyone.*[89] In the symbolic language he used, this meant, go forth with faithful confidence, drawing out of everyone you meet their own divine indwelling Christ light. It was his contribution to modern metaphysical Christianity that he should be the first to teach the Inner Light, which is Christ within.

George Fox lived in dangerous times. Those times were noteworthy for their singular lack of tolerance. Protestant and Catholic dynasties came and went, leaving the throne first in the hands of the "heretics" (Protestants), then in the grasp of the "papists" (Catholics), and then back to Protestant rule once again. In Fox's native England, it began a century before him with the most famous Henry of all.

Henry VIII had more problems than six wives to deal with during his reign of thirty-seven years at the beginning of the sixteenth century. He also had a revolution on his hands—a religious revolution. Martin Luther challenged papal authority and succeeded in convincing German princes that they would be better off keeping their taxes than sending them to Rome. Of course, there were deep religious and philosophical reasons for Luther's break with Roman Catholicism, but the economic factors helped him gain backing of powerful rulers and ensure the break with Roman Catholicism would not be quelled by armed might.

England's Henry Tudor, known to us as Henry VIII, wrote an attack on Luther in 1521 entitled "Assertion of the Seven Sacraments against Martin Luther." It was poorly constructed, containing mostly biblical quotes juxtaposed with relentless abuse. He wrote of Luther: *What serpent so venomous as he who calls the pope's authority tyrannous? ... What a great limb of the Devil is he, endeavoring to tear the Christian members of Christ from their head! ... the whole Church is subject not only to Christ but ... to Christ's vicar, the Pope of Rome.* [90]

Luther, no pushover when it came to controversy, replied in kind, calling Henry some rather unpleasant names. Luther's abuse even transcended Henry's: ... *that frantic madman ... the King of Lies ... by God's disgrace King of England ... Since with malice aforethought that damnable and rotten worm has lied against my King in heaven it is right for me to bespatter this English monarch with his own filth.* [91]

In Rome, the reigning Pope Leo X was cheered by Henry's frontal assault on Luther's teachings and character. Leo awarded the English king the title *Defensor Fidei,* Defender of the Faith. Later, when Henry broke with Rome over his attempt to divorce Catherine and marry Anne Boleyn, he would outlaw both Lutheranism and Catholicism, which prompted Luther to grumble: *This king wants to be God. He founds articles of faith, which even the Pope never did.* [92]

And all these groups busily set to work persecuting, flogging, attacking with armies, and burning each other at the stake. It was a tough time to be a common man, for you did not know which side to support or which form of religion to embrace. If you became an Anglican—that is, a member of the Protestant State Church founded by Henry—and the Catholics came to power, which they did when his daughter Mary took the throne, it could make things less than comfortable. Quite a few people converted to Catholicism during Mary's reign only to find themselves on the outside of the Establishment when her half-sister, Queen Elizabeth (who was Protestant), took over.

Those were times when a person could be hanged for the merest offense. Burning at the stake was the common lot for those who were found to be "heretics." A heretic? Anyone who disagrees with the fellow holding the matches to light the execution pyre. First, Henry was the Defender of the Faith, opponent of Protestantism. Then he was throwing off all Roman Catholic influences and establishing a Protestant church. It was a time when wise men kept silent about their religious convictions. As late as 1639 the government considered burning a tradesman as an example to other secret heretics. His offenses, one historian said, *The counts on which he was charged ... non-attendance at church, studying the Bible at home, being against printed prayers, and being opposed to the systems of bishops.*[93]

He was not burned, but he could have been. As most of us could have been, had we lived in his time and place.

It was into this mad, bloodthirsty religious whirlpool there walked a man of joy, peace, and boundless enthusiasm who would not be silent nor bow to anyone but his Lord. His name was George Fox.

We shall let his most famous convert introduce him to us. William Penn writes of his friend: *The blessed instrument ... of God ... of whom I am now about to write, was George Fox ... a worthy man, witness and servant of God in his time ... George Fox was born in Leicestershire, about the year 1624. He descended of honest and sufficient parents, who endeavored to bring him up ... in the way of the worship of the nation ....*[94]

That could only mean the Church of England, Anglicanism, or as we know it in the American continent, the Protestant Episcopal Church. During the reign of Queen Elizabeth I, Anglicanism became a state Protestant church which proudly charted a course in the "Middle Way," between Lutheranism and Catholicism. Church of England would be Lutheran in certain doctrines (such as justification by faith) and yet retain the Catholic system of bishops and a high church ritual quite similar to the Roman Catholic Mass. The primary difference was that now the head of the church was not the Pope but the ruling monarch.

In theory, Anglicanism saw itself as moderate, tolerant, willing to allow divergences of opinion. To be fair to the traditions of Episcopalianism, we should note that this really does characterize the general tone of the church down to this day: moderate liberalism in an open framework, undergirded by ancient ritual and a high view of the sacraments and ministry.

However, in the days of George Fox, tolerance found its definition in a much narrower context than today. In fact, the Church of England in its early stages was quite oppressive of anyone who did not conform to its teachings. These "non-conformists" as they were called, often found themselves jailed, their property confiscated, and sometimes their lives forfeited.

Everyone had to pay taxes. What people in the North American continent often fail to realize is that the tradition of Church and State as separate entities is not worldwide. Most European churches get operating money from general tax revenues. If your church was branded "heretical" by the government in power—as were all but the Anglican churches—that meant not only would your group be cut off from any government money to support your church, but it also meant that you would be taxed to support a church to which you did not subscribe. Your taxes would go in part to pay the salaries of Anglican clergy and provide upkeep on State Church buildings. Protestors to the system were jailed, beaten, and killed.

George Fox did not seem to notice the danger. Born of humble stock in a tiny village in Leicestershire, the young man seemed from the outset to be a spiritual seeker who questioned, wondered, and marveled at all he discovered. He used the quaint language of that era to describe his spiritual journeying, so as we look at his writings and experiences we shall have to rethink the definitions of certain words to understand what Fox said. (This is, incidentally, an equal problem we face when reading the archaic language of the King James Bible, translated in 1611, thirteen years before Fox was born.)

Young George Fox hungered for some kind of spiritual insight. He recorded his struggles in his "Journal," which has come down to us as one of the most remarkable spiritual autobiographies ever written: *I was about twenty years of age when these exercises (soul-searchings) came upon me; and some years I continued in that condition, in great trouble (distress); and fain I would have put it from me. I went to many a priest to look for comfort, but found no comfort from them.* [95]

He began his wanderings about this time, traveling on horseback and on foot. Later, he would travel by ship to spread his doctrine of peace and love to the West Indies and North America. He was a rugged man, enduring much physical suffering in the service of his Lord. He told of a night spent in the Americas when it was so cold that they made a fire in the woods to keep warm, but a basin of water near the fire froze solid before dawn. They slept on the ground that night, as they usually did. Fox wrote in his characteristic manner of understatement: *That night, also, we lay in the woods; and so extremely cold was the weather, the wind blowing high, and the frost and snow being great, that it was hard for some of us to abide it.* [96]

Yet, those days of zealous missionary activity were still in the future as young

George Fox roamed the hillsides of rural England in his quest for spiritual enlightenment during the early years of his adulthood. He often went to clergymen for help. But the institutional religion—which had grown up under Henry VIII and suffered through persecutions by one ruling party after another—bred men of the cloth who hesitated to give opinions on anything slightly controversial. George Fox brought them questions and problems of a deeply disturbing, provocative nature. He could get no member of the establishment clergy to discuss them with him.

He was discussing his plight with a cleric, named Dr. Cradock, walking in the afternoon sunlight through the clergyman's garden: *Now, as we were walking together in his garden, the alley being narrow, I chance, in turning, to set my foot on the side of a bed, at which the man was in a rage, as if his house had been on fire. Thus all our discourse was lost, and I went away in sorrow, worse than when I came.*[97]

One suspects when reading Fox's "Journal," that the Anglican clergy of that day had little training in counseling.

Confused but undaunted, George kept traveling in hopes of encountering someone who would enlighten him. In this, his story resembles the wanderings of the Buddha or the searching of Yogananda, or perhaps even the wilderness period early in the ministry of Jesus. Many great religious leaders—Moses, Mohammed, Bahaullah, Joseph Smith—had to go apart from the crowd and seek a vision of Truth which they would bring back from the wilderness to teach their fellow seekers.

For George Fox, his moment of enlightenment came on a quiet English hilltop. It was only after five years of wandering—meeting failure and despair, convincing a few people but suffering imprisonment twice for his incessant questioning—that Fox would come to his mature vision of what the ancient faith ought to be.

Dr. D. Elton Trueblood describes this experience in his book "The People Called Quakers:" *He climbed a hill on the border of Lancastershire and Yorkshire, part of the Pennine range, and there, on a beautifully clear day, arrived at a wholly new conception of his work in the world.*[98]

Fox describes the experience in his "Journal:" *As we travelled we came near a very great hill, called Pendle Hill, and I was moved of the Lord to go to the top of it; which I did with difficulty, it was so steep and high. When I was come to the top, I saw the sea bordering Lancastershire. From the top of this hill the Lord let me see in what places he had a great people to be gathered .... Christ was come to teach people Himself, by His power and Spirit in their hearts, and to bring people off from all the world's ways and teachers, to His own free teaching ....* [99]

What was this message George perceived? Dr. Martin Marty of the University of Chicago's Divinity School summarized it succinctly: *Christ lives in the inner man—only there.* [100]

He taught that religious Truth (he used capital T) must be proven in everyday life. He preached that all persons—men and women alike—have within them an inner light which can guide them, if they will listen to it. He identified this light with the spirit of Christ, which he said dwells in everyone.

Moreover, he insisted that it was not in external ceremonies and rituals that Truth could be known, but only through meditation and introspection. Only within us does divinity dwell, he said, not in temples made of stone by human hands.

He was certainly teaching nothing new;

Paul had told the Athenians much the same thing in his speech on Mars' Hill recorded in Acts 17:22-31. George Fox, however, had the temerity to believe it. He lived his life as though God's indwelling Spirit was readily available to him for continual guidance. He spoke frequently of "openings" or spiritual insights he gleaned almost daily.

A few passages from his "Journal" will illustrate the remarkable quality of George Fox's ceaseless communion with his inner Guide: *Now the Lord God opened to me by His invisible power that every man was enlightened by the divine Light of Christ, and I saw it shine through all; and that they that believed in it came out of condemnation to the Light of life, and became children of it.... On a certain time, as I was walking in the fields, the Lord said unto me, "Thy name is written in the Lamb's book of life, which was before the foundation of the world": and as the Lord spoke it, I believed, and saw in it the new birth.... Moreover, when the Lord sent me forth into the world, He forbade me to put off my hat to any, high or low; and I was required to Thee and Thou all men and women (that is, say "Thee" and "Thou" instead of "You"), without any respect to rich or poor, great or small.*[101]

Privileges of rank and title ruled the land in those days, yet George Fox and his swelling ranks of fellow-seekers refused to bow, scrape, or doff their hats to anyone. This managed to offend almost everyone, as George tells us: *Oh, the blows, punchings, beatings and imprisonments that we underwent for not putting off our hats to men! Some had their hats violently plucked off and thrown away, so that they quite lost them. The bad language and evil usage we received on this account are hard to be expressed, besides the danger we were sometimes in of losing our lives for this matter . . . .*[102]

Surely he is exaggerating?

Not one bit. Dutch theologian Henry Van Etten describes the kind of reception Quakerism received in the New World during Fox's lifetime: *Persecution was fierce: they were expelled from Boston, and they were threatened with death if they returned to Massachusetts; but they returned. Four of them were executed at Boston between 1659 and 1661; one of these, Mary Dyer, who had been pardoned the previous year, was hanged because she had come back a third time.*[103]

George Fox suffered numerous imprison-

ments, too. There was a standing order that
every English subject could be required to
take an oath of loyalty to the King. This oath
had to be sworn in public upon a Bible.
"Friends," as the Quakers began to call
themselves, refused to take an oath because
of the teaching of Jesus in Matthew 5:34-37.
This led an already critical government to believe that these gentle Quakers, who called
themselves "Children of the Light," were disloyal, rebellious, and plotting to overthrow
the government.

England had just gone through a revolution and counter-revolution. King Charles I
was beheaded, and Oliver Cromwell became
dictator of the nation without a king. Cromwell's republic died with him, and the Stuart
restoration brought Charles II to the throne
in 1660, during the height of Fox's activism.
An already nervous government, besieged
with plots by Catholics and radical Protestants to set up their form of theocratic
government, established a loyalty oath that
all subjects could be required to affirm on
pain of imprisonment.

However, the Friends refused to swear any
oath. Many of them went to jail for their
belief. We have a remarkable record of such a

trial in Fox's "Journal." Admittedly a one-sided report, it nevertheless gives insight into the period.

Fox was arraigned on charges of refusing to swear the loyalty oath. After a mistrial, he was declared free, but the judge put the oath to him once more. Fox was handed a Bible and directed to swear the oath upon it. The reply he gave was: *Then said I, 'Ye have given me a book here to kiss and swear on, and this book which ye have given me to kiss says, 'Kiss the Son;' and the Son says in this book, 'Swear not at all;' and so says the apostle James. Now, I say as the book says, and yet ye imprison me; why do ye not imprison the book for saying so?'*[104]

Fox was so persuasive that the judge admitted he wished the law were otherwise. He sent George to jail.

Another element in Quaker belief which caused such a stir was their radical universalism, that is, their acceptance of other people as having the Inner Light, too. Even Puritans, who accepted the idea that revelation outside the Bible was possible, found this idea loathsome. After all, if our Truth conflicts with your Truth, how can you be right? Fox insisted that Truth was one, and yet there could be different viewpoints. He accepted the Inner Light in all people—slaves and freedmen, Indians, Muslims, and all other Christian denominations. He wrote: *. . . and this I knew experimentally.* [105]

The result of such open-mindedness can be seen in the demographics of colonial America. Puritan New England allowed immigrants, at first, from only sects like their own. Quaker Pennsylvania welcomed everyone—Jews, Catholics, Anglicans, Mennonites, Moravians, and others. Boston had its executions for heresy; Philadelphia flourished as a multicultural center where the radicals of another age would guarantee freedom of belief for all. [106]

George Fox laid the groundwork for all Inner Light teachers who came after him. He denied that authority was external, insisting on the promptings of the Spirit within every person. Fox read the Bible, but reserved the right to interpret it in the light of his inner Guide, the Christ wihin. His influence and the influence of the *Society of Friends* (or *Quakers* as they were called because of their fervor) remains with us today. They are still walking cheerfully over the Earth in his footsteps.

In his seeking, he anticipated Charles Fillmore's own quest. Fox found no satisfaction in the confusion of religious sects endemic to seventeenth-century England. Like Fillmore, he decided that in this babble he would "go to headquarters," he would look for God's guidance within him. Modern mystical/metaphysical Christianity may give thanks to divine order that he found what he was searching for—Christ within us all.

Yet there were still questions to be addressed. If God is in everything, why is there apparent evil? Can a religious system really affirm God's goodness when faced with the catastrophic events of human history? Another European thinker would supply some of the answers. The gears set in motion by early mystical theologians were about to be retooled into an intricate, exhaustive thought system by one of the greatest philosophers of all time.

8

First, Second, and Third Force George Wilhelm Friedrich Hegel (1770-1831)

In the chapter "Understanding" from Charles Fillmore's *The Twelve Powers of Man*, he makes this important distinction: *There are two schools of writers on metaphysical subjects... First are those who handle the mind and its faculties from an intellectual standpoint, among whom may be mentioned Kant, Hegel, Mill, Schopenhauer, and Sir William Hamilton. The other school includes all the great company of religious authors who have discerned that Spirit and soul are the causing factors of the mind.*[107]

Fillmore correctly observed that, in his

day, there were those who proposed spiritual intuition as the basis for Truth. These would follow in the footsteps of men like George Fox, the founder of the Quaker movement, who believed the Inner Light was the only source of Truth. Yet, there was another group who taught ideas similar to Unity, metaphysical thinkers who used the tools of philosophy to arrive at similar conclusions. We have looked at people with both viewpoints in our study.

The names Fillmore mentions are given without explanation. Note that there is only one full name in the list. Charles Fillmore assumed his readers knew who these men were and therefore they needed no introduction. However, the climate in which the Fillmores did their pioneering work—the latter part of the nineteenth century and the first decades of the twentieth—was a different world than today. In this study we will examine how that environment promoted the growth of metaphysical Christianity by investigating the lifework of one of the men mentioned by Fillmore, one of those "writers on metaphysical subjects" whom the founders of Unity assumed were famous enough to warrant no introduction.

Unity is a mature movement within liberal Protestantism, but it did not just materialize from the rare air of late nineteenth-century American religious thought. Our studies thus far have shown that the theology and practices we know as metaphysical Christianity are really long-standing beliefs of major thinkers throughout the course of Christian history.

Georg Wilhelm Friedrich Hegel was an intellectual giant who altered the intellectual climate of western society from an arid mechanical desert to a spirit-based hothouse where a riot of growth could occur. When he died of cholera in 1831 at the age of sixty-one, Hegel had succeeded in changing the way most educated Europeans looked at their world. His ideas would find their way to America soon, where Ralph Waldo Emerson and Theodore Parker would give them new vigor, providing an intellectual base for the developing New Thought Christian movement. And Hegel did all this work while Europe convulsed in the Napoleonic Wars, achieving a full-time university teaching position only after he was forty-six years old.

Hegel wrote in German, that marvelous language of precise phrases and freight-train nouns. Even so, Hegel wrote obscurely. He is difficult to read in translation and not much better in the original. The vast scope of his philosophy makes it difficult for anyone outside the Hegelian *weltanschauung* (worldview) to grasp what his logical mind is saying.

Coming to the Hegelian philosophy for the first time is like discovering a great, whistling, bleeping machine busily chugging away at whatever it is doing. We see order, precision. We are sure it must be doing something because there is coordinated movement of parts. However, until we find some kind of operating instructions or blueprints to explain what the thing does, we can make no sense out of the whirling gears and flashing lights before us. That is an outsider's impression of Hegel's philosophy.

Our first instinct might be to turn and leave, because it will require some head-scratching and hard work to ponder the functions of the beast before us. But somehow we suspect the beast is hiding within its form a handsome prince with the keys to a kingdom of new awareness. Hegel is too important to flee from, too deep to wade through, too vast to go around. We must approach the philosophy before us and work at understanding its complexity. There is no other way to understand the origins of modern metaphysical Christianity.

So far-reaching is the Hegelian worldview that its American counterparts, transcendentalism and absolute idealism, became the unchallenged school of philosophy taught by colleges and universities in North America until after World War I. The teachers who founded virtually every modern metaphysical Christian movement come from a Hegelian approach to reality. Those teachers include Charles and Myrtle Fillmore.

Because Hegel's thought and the works of those who built on his system dominated their era, pioneers like Charles Fillmore assumed we would understand the Hegelian worldview and seldom saw a need to explain the traditional philosophical position of their time. Explaining Hegel for turn-of-the-century metaphysical Christians would be like explaining electricity under the lights of a night baseball game. We take Edison's discovery for granted, just as they took absolute idealism for granted when Unity was in its infancy. Today Hegelianism is out of fashion, so we must rediscover the view our recent spiritual forefathers accepted so readily. When we find the blueprints for Hegelianism, some of the obscure passages in early metaphysical writing become much more intelligible.

Hegel was a philosopher, not a theologian. A philosopher may or may not be a practicing believer. Philosophy supposedly begins at a point and proceeds logically to wherever truth may lead the philosopher. No ideas are allowed to stand unless they meet the strictest standards. Philosophy owes no allegiance to any prophet, concept, person, or revealed religion. It is, in theory, empirical.

Theology, on the other hand, begins within the circle of faith. A Jewish theologian will deal with concepts native to Jewish thought; a Muslim theologian will investigate the ideas and central themes of Islam. If the Muslim thinker ever came to the conclusion that Judaism is true and Islam false, he would no longer be a Muslim theologian. Theology, therefore, is logical reflection on widely-believed categories within a community of faith. Philosophy is individual investigation which may or may not be shared by any other person or community.

Many early theologians used philosophical

tools and were often quite aware of the contributions of philosophy to clarifying the beliefs of their community of faith. Hegel is purely a philosopher. Yet his conclusions sound quite "theological" because he answered questions about how reality hangs together: what is real and unreal, and what part God plays in our study of life. In the language of philosophy, these are all metaphysical questions.

Hegel believed that there is one absolute power. He called this omnipresent power by the German word *geist*, which can be translated *spirit* or *mind*. We recognize the same root word in *geist* from which the modern English noun *ghost* derives. Hegel did not mean *ghost*, unless we employ the archaic use of that word (as for example, the Holy Ghost is the Holy Spirit). For Hegel, everything is part of Spirit. Spirit manifests itself by creating the physical universe. This Spirit he readily identified with intelligence, Divine Mind. He believed that Mind is so potent that it creates the reality around us. Hegel did not go so far as to suggest that the things around us—chairs, trees, kites, and koalas—are not really there. For him, what is really there is what we see, and by our seeing it, it becomes real. Confusing? Here is an example:

If we very firmly believe that we are sickly, weak, and frail, we shall outpicture these infirmities. This is a basic belief of most metaphysical Christians. Why is this so? Hegel would assert that this is so because we are spirit, and spirit has the power to shape reality. In fact, spirit is the true nature of all that is. Spirit is the energy source which causes everything to be. Matter does not contain spirit; matter exists because spirit empowers it, much like a movie projector empowers rivers and mountains to exist on a screen. Except that for Hegel, spirit makes not images, but reality. Spirit is the key to Hegel's system.

It is impossible to comprehensively deal with a thinker as profound as Hegel in a short article. Therefore, we shall touch briefly upon two aspects of his system which most directly influence modern thought in general and Unity's theological heritage in particular: Hegelian monism and the dialectic (thesis, antithesis, synthesis). Hegel's contribution to our approach to religion would be profound if these were all he had to say, so we shall concentrate on them.

Hegelian monism. Hegel was an idealist,

which is a word used differently in philosophy than in everyday English. Perhaps it is better to think of it here as "idea-ism."

Idealism holds that the true reality of all things is not matter but the power which generates matter, Spirit. Thus it is the polar opposite of *materialism*. Materialism asserts that the only reality that exists is the physical world as it appears to us through our senses. This dichotomy between idealism and materialism explains some of the tirades against "sense consciousness" in early metaphysical Christian writers since it was the materialists who denied that anything could be known that was not known through sensory input. This was their ploy to deny that anything spiritual exists.

Carried to its logical conclusion, idealism—the belief that Spirit empowers all that exists—leads directly to *monism*, which is the view that there is only one Power and Presence in the universe, Divine Mind. Monism, however, is a difficult belief to maintain in the face of everyday reality. If only God, the good exists, why is there suffering in the world? Why are there hungry children, battered wives, poor people, victims of war and crime and disease?

This problem is called *theodicy*. It may be the oldest religious problem known to humanity, and there are no neat answers to it. Monism, in its radical form, sweeps aside the reality of suffering by denying that anything but good can happen. Thus radical monism sacrifices the right to feel pain when we hurt for the sake of a theological concept which denies that pain exists.

Yet, *dualism*—which asserts that there are two powers, one good and one evil—is even less satisfying. Daniel Defoe pointed out the absurdity of dualism in his classic novel "Robinson Crusoe." Crusoe instructs the so-called savage he named "Friday" in the subtleties of dualistic religion: *After this, I had been telling him how the Devil was God's enemy in the hearts of men, and used all his malice and skill to defeat the good designs of Providence, and to ruin the kingdom of Christ in the world, and the like. "Well," says Friday, "but you say God is so strong, so great; is he not much strong, much might as the Devil?—"Yes, yes," says I, "Friday, God is stronger than the Devil; God is above the Devil . . . . " "But," says he again, "if God much stronger, much might as the Devil, why God not kill the Devil, so make him no more do wicked?*"[108] Crusoe changes the subject. He is unable to deal with this question even though it comes from the lips of a "savage."

This, then, is the dilemma: to affirm dualism leaves one without a unifying factor in the universe, makes God responsible for evil because theoretically He could end it all by killing the devil, as Friday suggests.

However, monism in its radical form is unsatisfying, too, because it denies the everyday experience of pain, suffering, and struggle we see around us.

Is there a way to maintain the unity of monism—the belief in one Power and Presence—without denying that anyone suffers? Hegel believed he had found the answer. And even philosophers who do not like his conclusion have marveled at how cogently Hegel argues his case. Dr. John MacQuarrie wrote this description of the Hegelian system: *Hegel was not only an idealist but also a monist, that is to say, he held that reality is one. But this unity does not preclude difference. Rather, the development of the absolute spirit involves differentiation, but such a way that the differences are held together in a more comprehensive unity. . . . For Hegel, reality is so much a unity that no individual fact can be fully understood except in its relation to the whole.*[109]

Putting this in ordinary language, contrast is necessary in order for us to have any concept whatsoever. Good is the only reality, but it cannot be appreciated unless it is contrasted with its absence, which we call evil.

H. Emilie Cady put it this way: *Apparent evils are not entities or things of themselves. They are simply apparent absence of the good, just as darkness is an absence of light.*[110]

Charles Fillmore adds this: *Evil is a parasite. It has no permanent life of itself; its whole existence depends on the life it borrows from its parent, and when its connection with the parent is severed, nothing remains. In Divine Mind there is no recognition of evil conditions.... Apparent evil is the result of ignorance and when Truth is presented the error disappears.*[111]

How, then, do we explain existential evil encountered in everyday life? Hegel has a practical, ingenious method of incorporating the nonexistence of evil (monism) into a worldview which does not try to deny that people hurt other people or that tragedy does occur. This is the blueprint we have been seeking to understand the Hegelian *weltan-schauung*. It is called in philosophy the *dialectic* or *thesis-antithesis-synthesis*. In recent years, it has become popularly known to metaphysical students as *First, Second, and Third Force*.

The Dialectic. We noted that good, which is the only reality, cannot be understood except in contrast. Because we have known both good and un-good, we know goodness. If we take light and dark or heat and cold for examples, the problem becomes clearer.

Imagine a world with two suns where there is never night. On that world the people would, of course, have no conception of darkness. However, they would also have no concept of day. We know daylight only by its contrast, night. And even though there is only power involved here—that of sunlight and its absence—a contrast is not only helpful but absolutely necessary. The same would be true of heat and its absence, cold.

In other words, heat and cold are not two concepts at war with each other but a single concept producing a third state called aware-ness of temperature. The same is true of good and its absence, un-good or evil, which pro-duce the third state called freedom. If we were incapable of choosing un-good, we would not be free.

This is the famous Hegelian dialectic: thesis, antithesis, and synthesis. MacQuarrie describes it thus: *As development produces differentiation, the differences conflict, but in truth they are complementary, and are reconciled in a higher unity . . . Hegelian Dialectic, whereby the conflict of thesis and antithesis is resolved in a higher synthesis.*[112]

Charles Fillmore added this in *Mysteries of Genesis: "Good and evil," primarily representing two poles of Being, are opposite but not adverse to each other.*[113]

Another version of the Hegelian dialectic has found its way into twentieth-century metaphysical Christianity through the difficult to obtain and even more difficult to understand five-volume series on "The Work" (of G. I. Gurdjieff and P. D. Ouspensky), given originally as lectures by Maurice Nicoll. A central concept of "The Work" which has become somewhat popular is known as the "Law of the Three." You will immediately recognize it as Hegelianism: *Every manifestation in the Universe is a result of the combination of three forces. These forces are called Active Force, Passive*

Force, and Neutralizing Force. Active Force is called 1st Force, Passive Force is called 2d Force, Neutralizing Force is called 3d Force.[114]

When we begin a project or step out on any new venture, from launching a new career to leaving the house to catch a bus in the morning, the energy we employ to obtain our objectives is 1st Force (thesis). As soon as we set forth, we immediately encounter resistance, problems of how to get that job or catch that bus, which is 2d Force (antithesis). If we persevere, we shall combine our efforts with the experiences of resistance and come up with a result, 3d Force (synthesis).

The practical aspect of this philosophy is that it gives us a way of looking at obstacles and resistance while maintaining a positive consciousness. Nicoll said: *These three forces are found in Nature and in Man. Throughout the Universe, on every plane, these three forces are at work. They are the creative forces. Nothing is produced without the conjunction of these three forces. The conjunction of these three forces constitutes a triad.*[115]

Hegel believed that reality is arranged in these triads. He saw the dialectic operating throughout time, as the outpouring of Spirit continued to create, continued evolving the universe. Hegelian thought is a metaphysical system, in that it attempts to explain how reality fits together, and a practical system, because it insists that truth is known only in concrete terms, in everyday experiences. We learn about good from the experience of the good in life, not from abstract speculation, Hegel would insist.

Hegel was optimistic about our ability to comprehend, albeit in a limited way, the things of God. In one of the few unobtrusive passages from "Philosophy of History," Hegel waxes poetic in an ode to Christian seeking: *In the Christian religion God has revealed Himself, that is, He has given us to understand what He is; so that He is no longer a concealed or secret existence. And this possibility of knowing Him, thus afford-ed us, renders such knowledge a duty. God wishes no narrow-hearted souls or empty heads for His children; but those whose spirit is of itself indeed, poor, but rich in the knowl-edge of Him; and who regard this knowledge of God as the only valuable possession.*[116]

He did not originate the concept of triadic reality. This can be traced as far back as

Proclus (fifth century A.D.) and before him in Christian and Hindu theologies of the Trinity. Hegel popularized the dialectic and the notion that underlying all reality there is one unifying principle, Divine Mind. He led the way for Gurdjieff and Ouspensky and their popularizer Maurice Nicoll to show how the dialectic applied to everyday life as 1st, 2d, and 3d Force. He gave German idealism its most comprehensive expression, which would cross the Atlantic and find its way into the works of nineteenth-century transcendentalists like Emerson and Parker, and thus into the fabric of Unity.

Georg Wilhelm Friedrich Hegel—struggling with great cosmic systems while Napoleon's cannons rolled across Europe—laid the foundation for modern metaphysical Christianity.

9

The Bridge Builders
Ralph Waldo Emerson
(1803-1882)
and
Theodore Parker
(1810-1860)

Man is the wonderworker. He is seen amid miracles... refuse the good models, even those which are sacred in the imagination of men, and dare to love God without mediator or veil.... Yourself a new-born bard of the Holy Ghost,—cast behind you all conformity, and acquaint men at first hand with Deity.[117]
Ralph Waldo Emerson, "The Divinity School Address"

The end of Christianity seems to be to make all men one with God as Christ was one with him; to bring them to such a state of obedience and goodness that we shall think divine thoughts and feel divine sentiments .... It does not demand all men to think alike, but to think uprightly, and get near as possible at truth....[118] Theodore Parker, "The Transient and Permanent in Christianity"

Rarely do the giants among us collaborate or even converse, perhaps because they have their own worlds to live in and their own spheres of influence. However, there is a record of a confrontation between two great religious leaders that took place five hundred years before the birth of Jesus Christ. It was at the huge Imperial Library of China in the city of Loyang that two men who were destined to be founders of two faiths (which would eventually claim millions of devotees) met face-to-face.

Lao-tzu, father of Taoism, clashed in debate with Kung-Fu-tzu, known to the western world as Confucius. They represented two radically different approaches to everyday life. Lao-tzu was the ascetic, the one who exhorted followers to withdraw from the world and contemplate the divine way, the Tao. Confucius, on the other hand, believed that involvement in the world was the way to a better world for all.

Two exchanges from their debate suffice to give us a good summary of their positions: *"One should contemplate the meaning of death,"* Lao-tzu said, *"and the way of the divine."* Confucius replied: *"How can one know anything about death when we know so little about life? They that teach of the gods are often ignorant of human ways."*[119]

This simple point-and-counterpoint between two of humanity's greatest religious teachers draws a good contrast. What is the goal of true religion? For some it is self-centered, and "self-centered" as it is used here does not mean "selfish." Self-centered religion concerns itself with individual spirituality through good works, faith, acts of piety, meditation, prayer, and a host of other techniques. The goal of this first kind of religion, that advocated by Lao-tzu, is individual salvation. It begins and ends with the individual, and therefore does nothing by itself to promote the general good of all humanity.

Although there are many passages in the New Testament which suggest the individual must *"seek first the Kingdom of God,"* there is another voice to be heard along the path to individual "salvation" or Christ-consciousness. It is the voice of the poor, the oppressed, the hungry, the sick, the downtrodden. Jesus was explicit about the commitment He expected His followers to have in regard to these, "the least" among us. Yet, throughout history, there has been a longstanding debate between the "Taoist" and "Confucianist" people of all religions. Some say we need to find our own spiritual path and that will soon enough change the world. Others believe that anyone who is truly on the path of enlightenment will find it impossible to progress down that path with the sick, the hungry, and the destitute strewn along the way. For this latter group, spirituality is always a call to make this world a better place by doing unto others what we would want done unto us.

Two great American religious thinkers represent this clash of theories. They are the subject of this study, the first one to leap across the ocean from the Old World to the new and deal with theologians who are part of our American heritage and our Unity ancestry. One needs practically no introduction. Ralph Waldo Emerson is required reading in nearly every school district in the United

States and quite a few in Canada as well. He has been called the "American Shakespeare," and has the distinction of being the author most frequently quoted by Charles Fillmore, with the exception of Shakespeare. Emerson is quoted by more Unity writers than any other religious author of previous eras. In her book, *Lessons in Truth,* Dr. H. Emilie Cady mentions Emerson's work six times.

Theodore Parker is less known, although his work receives mention in classes taught at Unity Village. Parker was a young contemporary of Emerson who knew the great lecturer and essayist personally and who carried into action some of Emerson's theoretical notions.

In this study we shall look at these two men who are an important bridge in the history of Unity School of Christianity. They provided the Fillmores with a theological/theoretical basis for the emerging Unity movement. But they also provide us with a bridge backward to our own past, the long heritage of original thinkers and doers who have caught a glimpse of the divine oneness and passed that vision along to those of us who have come after them. Emerson and Parker are the missing link that ties

nineteenth-century New Thought Christianity with mainline Protestant thought, for we
most certainly can claim these two giants as
our antecedents in the search for practical
Christian truths.

Emerson was born in Boston on May 25,
1803. He came from a long line of ministers
and scholars. His father was pastor of First
Church, Boston, but died in 1811, leaving the
mother to struggle to support the children.
Emerson was a bright boy so he attended
Latin School as a youth and then Harvard
College. He went on to Harvard Divinity
School but never graduated. He was ordained
a Unitarian minister and served as pastor of
Second Church in Boston for about three
years. When his wife, Ellen, died, he resigned
his post and sailed for Europe where he spent
almost a year.

When he returned, Emerson turned to lecturing and writing full time. He did some sub-
stitute preaching but never again held a par-
ish ministry. His second marriage endured
the rest of his long life. Lydia Jackson Emerson gave him three children, one who died at
five years old. Emerson was to write moving-
ly about this tragedy in a poem entitled
"Threnody." Here is a brief passage which

captures the melancholy of this time in his life:

> *O child of paradise,*
> *Boy who made dear his father's home,*
> *In whose deep eyes*
> *Men read the welfare of times to come,*
> *I am too much bereft.*
> *The world dishonored thou hast left.*[120]

Emerson recovered from the tragedy, publishing his "Second Series" of essays and fathering another son, Edward Waldo, two years later.

Perhaps his greatest contribution to American Christianity came about as the result of his growing fame as a lecturer. In the spring of 1838 he received an invitation from a committee of the senior class at Harvard Divinity School to speak there.

He was struggling with the concept of "ministry" at the time, so he used the occasion as a place to air his views on the state of Christianity in general and the ministry in particular. On a clear, warm Boston evening he stood before an unsuspecting audience and delivered a lengthy sermon which has been called one of the most important Sunday messages given in modern times. It was an untitled lecture/sermon which has since come to be known simply as "The Divinity School Address." Protestant Christianity has never been the same.

What was the message Emerson preached that lazy summer evening almost a century and a half ago? He took the themes of German idealism (which we saw in our study of Hegel) and its American offshoot, transcendentalism, applying them to the teaching of Christian Truth for the New Age. Earl Morse Wilbur gives a summary of Emerson's remarks in his book "Our Unitarian Heritage":
He (Emerson) complained that the prevailing religion of the day had little life or inspiration in it because it was forever looking to persons and events in the past history of Christianity, rather than listening to hear what God has to say to men today; and he urged them not to attach importance to miracles ... but to seek the truths of religion within their own souls, and to preach to men what God reveals to them there. Thus religion should be no longer cold and formal, but a vital personal experience.[121]

Even more importantly, Emerson insisted that what Jesus *was* we shall become. He denied the unique divinity of Jesus but saw Him as the Way-Shower for all humanity to realize its oneness with God. In powerful phrases shaped by the finest theological writer of the nineteenth century, Ralph Waldo Emerson foreshadowed the whole vast scope of modern practical Christianity when he spoke these words that night in the Divinity School Chapel at Harvard: "*Jesus Christ belonged to the true race of prophets. He saw with open eye the mystery of the soul. Drawn by its severe harmony, ravished with its beauty, he lived in it, and had his being there. Alone in history, he estimated the greatness of man. One man was true to what is in you and me. He saw that God incarnates himself in man, and evermore goes forth anew to take possession of his world. He said, in his jubilee of sublime emotion, 'I am divine. Through me, God acts; through me, speaks. Would you see God, see me; or, see thee, when thou also thinkest as I now think.'*"[122]

Emerson was already in enough trouble with the more traditionally minded members of the congregation, although the graduating students and young visiting ministers were on the edge of their chairs by now. Having gone this far, the bard of Concord followed his line of thought to its logical conclusion in a searing indictment of the state that

nineteenth-century Christianity had degen-
erated into: *"But what a distortion did his
doctrine and memory suffer in the same, in
the next, and the following ages! The understanding caught this high chant from the
poet's lips, and said, in the next age, 'This
was Jehovah come down out of heaven. I will
kill you if you say he was a man.' The idioms
of his language, and the figures of his
rhetoric, have usurped the place of his truth;
and churches are not built on his principle,
but on his tropes (figures of speech)."*[123]

Emerson went further still, proclaiming
that everything Jesus taught was natural,
not supernatural. Miracles do exist, but not
as supernatural interventions into time and
space. Those things we call miracles are
operating on principles of divine law which
we do not yet understand. Emerson said: *"He
(Jesus) spoke of miracles; for he felt that
man's life was a miracle, and all that man
doth, and he knew that this daily miracle
shines, as the character ascends. But the
word miracle, as pronounced by Christian
churches, gives a false impression; it is
Monster. It is not one with the blowing clover
and the falling rain."*[124]

It is important that we pause here and

remember that Ralph Waldo Emerson regarded himself a Christian and probably as a Christian minister following a different calling. He is not opposed to Christianity, nor to the Christian churches. What Emerson was saying was that he believed the person and miracles of Jesus were set on so lofty a pedestal that no mere mortal could ever hope to achieve what Jesus did. It was not the divinity of Jesus that Emerson challenged; it was the uniqueness of that divinity. He believed we all have within us the same imprint of divinity, that Jesus is special because: *"Alone in human history, he estimated the greatness of man.... He saw that God incarnates himself in man, and evermore goes forth anew to take possession of his world."*[125]

So miracles—supernatural intervention into time and space by a divine agency—were unnecessary for Emerson. Those things we call miraculous are just powers of our Christ-nature that we all possess yet few of us manifest. If we all possess the divine nature, what can be better than to go within and seek Truth from our own inner guide? And when we find that Truth, then we join in community with other seeking souls and engage in the dialectical process of sharing, comparing what we have learned.

In one evening Ralph Waldo Emerson had struck down the long-held position of even his liberal Christian colleagues that the chief evidences for Christianity were the miracles and the uniqueness of Jesus Christ. Emerson turned that inside out and affirmed that the best in Christianity shows how very normal Jesus Christ was: *"That which shows God in me, fortifies me. That which shows God out of me, makes me a wart and a wen. There is no longer a necessary reason for my being. Already the long shadows of untimely oblivion creep over me, and I shall decease forever.... The time is coming when all men will see, that the gift of God to the soul is not a vaunting, over-powering, excluding sanctity, but a sweet, natural goodness, a goodness like thine and mine, and that so invites thine and mine to be and grow."*[126]

One of the young ministers who came to hear "The Divinity School Address" took up this challenge and committed himself to it the rest of his life. He was Theodore Parker, grandson of Captain John Parker who led the Yankee forces at the first skirmish of the Revolutionary War, Lexington, and may well have been the one who fired that "shot heard 'round the world." Parker reported in his letters and correspondence that grandfather John Parker was told by some of the men that they did not like the odds at Lexington (900 redcoats to Parker's 70 patriots) and wanted to flee. Captain Parker promptly drew his sword and vowed to run the first man through who even considered bolting his battle line. This action, it seems, was typical of the Parker family, because his grandson Theodore drew his sword-like pen and vowed eternal hostility toward anyone who supported the horrible institution which infected nineteenth-century America, human slavery.

Parker wrote his sermons with a gun on his desk because his home was a station in the underground railroad. Many times the Reverend Theodore Parker stood in danger of committing acts of violence even as he wrote words of love. He often had black families in his basement. The Fugitive Slave Law made it a crime for Parker to protect runaway slaves.

These were terrible times for American democracy. Theodore Parker would not sit idly by while his black brothers and sisters were hunted down by his white brothers and sisters. Here is a sample of his vehement denunciation of the law which made slaves no more than property and required all people to help slave owners retrieve their lost "merchandise": *The Fugitive Slave Bill is one of the most iniquitous statutes enacted in our time; it is only fit to be broken. In the name of justice, I call upon all men who love the law, to violate and break this Fugitive Slave Bill* . . . .[127]

Theodore Parker found Emerson's "Divinity School Address" . . . *the noblest, the most inspiring strain I ever listened to.*[128] But he did not just go home with a head full of new ideas; he put transcendentalism to work in everyday life. Parker truly believed that the divine was within all of us, so he became a fierce opponent of slavery. He saw Truth as one, so he began to study widely and even read eastern philosophies and religious works from non-Christian cultures. He was a committed follower of Jesus Christ, so he was not afraid to follow the path of Truth wherever it led him.

Parker was to Emerson as Confucius was to Lao-tzu. Emerson was a scholar, a thinker who wove words into tapestries of thought that enriched everyone who heard him. H. Emilie Cady wrote of him: *Emerson was a*

man of large individuality, but retiring per-
sonality. He was grandly simple. He was of a
shrinking, retiring nature (or personality).
But just in proportion as the human side of
him was willing to retire and be thought little
of, did the immortal, the God in him, shine
forth in greater degree.[129]

Emerson hated controversy and was
known for his mildness. He never criticized
anyone directly, although he had some problems with a minister or two as recorded in
Emerson's "Journals." One time when he
spoke at Middlebury, Vermont, a clergyman
came to the pulpit and delivered this closing
prayer: *We beseech thee, O Lord, to deliver us*
from hearing any more such transcendental
nonsense as we have just listened to from this
sacred desk.[130] Emerson leaned over to the
man next to him and asked the pastor's
name. He then remarked, gently, "He seemed
a very conscientious, plain-spoken man."
Nothing more was said in the face of such
attacks.

Parker, on the other hand, was a lion. He
roared about social issues; he railed against
slavery. He pushed for women's rights in the
1840s! He chided religious people for refusing
to do anything about the poor, the hungry,

the oppressed in the world.

In May 1841, Theodore Parker was invited to give the ordination address at Hawes Place Church, Boston, on the ordination to the Christian ministry of Reverend Charles C. Shackford. This address, coupled with Emerson's Divinity School piece, constitutes a rallying-point for nineteenth-century transcendentalism and its successor, New Thought Christianity. Parker said, clearly and in ringing terms, that there are those elements in every religion which must be viewed as passing fancies. He said there are deeper spiritual truths which must be culled from the pages of sacred scripture and a life of individual piety and prayer. He called his two-hour sermon "The Transient and Permanent in Christianity." Even today it reads fresh and vibrant, a monument to this rabble-rousing genius who pioneered a universalist approach to Truth from both east and west. Wilbur describes the central themes in Parker's message: *The permanent element in (Christianity)... is the teaching of Jesus, and the truth of that is self-evident apart from miracles; it does not rest on the personal authority of Jesus, indeed it would still remain true though it were proved that Jesus never lived at all. On the other hand, the forms and doctrines of Christianity are transient, changing from year to year....*[131]

In Parker's own text: *Jesus tells us, his word is the word of God, and so shall never pass away. But who tells us, that* our *word shall never pass away? that* our notion *of his Word shall stand forever.*[132]

Parker was refused fellowship by many of his brother ministers because of these "radical" views, which today seem rather tame. Nevertheless, he continued struggling for his vision of a Christian faith grounded in the teachings of Jesus but free from the bounds of superstition, free to explore new thoughts in the light of new discoveries of the modern age.

Emerson and Parker built bridges between the Old World and the New Age. They stood at the door to modern life and pointed the way for those who would come after them. Insisting on truth instead of dogma, justice instead of blind obedience, they were two modern prophets who created the kind of climate in which New Thought Christianity could flourish.

Although Emerson is regarded as the great genius, the finest author of his generation,

Parker in many ways surpassed Emerson's abilities. Parker studied and achieved competence in a phenomenal number of foreign languages: Italian, Portuguese, Dutch, Icelandic, Chaldaic, Arabic, Persian, Coptic, Aethiopic, Russian, Swedish, and of course the classical tongues of Latin, Greek, and Hebrew![133] An able speaker, perhaps the finest preacher of his day, he also wrote poetry which rivaled Emerson's best verse. The last two stanzas of his poem "Evening" serve both as an example of the deep feeling of this man and as a summary of his highest hopes for humankind:

> *Oh, night and stars! your voice I hear*
> *Swell round the listening pole:*
> *Your hymns are praises, loud and clear,*
> *Are music to my soul.*
>
> *Sing on, sing on, celestial band,*
> *Till earth repeats your lays,*
> *Till the wide sea, the sky, the land,*
> *Shall celebrate His praise![134]*

Ralph Waldo Emerson, the American Shakespeare, and his younger companion Theodore Parker were two men who struggled for new ideas and tried to live them in the real world. They were champions of the ancient faith who insisted on the right of every person to become what God intended him or her to be, a "new-born bard of the Holy Ghost." Emerson was the scholar, the gentle giant who tried to influence his world by example and quiet reflection. Parker was the activist who grappled with the evils of the day, who led the fight against slavery and cried like a lone voice in the wilderness for women's rights, the universality of Truth, the essential oneness of all humanity.

Did they resolve for us the ancient dialectic between Lao-tzu and Confucius? Not really. However, they showed by their very lives that it is possible to be a spiritual person who nonetheless takes an active part in the world. We might say that Emerson was a kind of American Taoist who still managed to change his world, and that Parker was a Yankee Confucianist who gave us deep insights into the divine. In true Hegelian fashion, they represented a thesis-antithesis which resolved itself in the synthesis of developing practical Christianity.

These two prophets of modern liberal Christianity give us reason to be proud of our heritage. The courage and ringing Truth of their lives is a tribute to the ancient faith.

Now we must leave the founders of modern mystical/metaphysical Christianity and move on into the twentieth century. The final section of this study will look at three women who launched great Truth movements still with us today, plus two theologians whose thinking shapes present mainline theology and who may hold the key to new theologies yet to come.

Part IV

Yesterday, Today, and Tomorrow

10

Three Women Prophets
Mary Baker Eddy
(1821-1910)
Emma Curtis Hopkins
(1853-1925)
Nona Brooks
(1866-1945)

I love to tell of the blessed change in outlook that came to us; of our remarkable healing; of the quick improvement of the financial situation. In fact our entire lives were transformed. We were thrilled! Who would not be![135] Nona Brooks, "Divine Science."

Early Christianity had a sour reputation in the Hellenistic world for a number of reasons. After all, these Christians were known atheists—they didn't believe in the gods! They refused to salute the Emperor's statue by offering wine and incense as a sacrifice in worship of Caesar. They were seditious and sneaky, meeting in private cells of subversives where they ate bodies and drank blood in their communion meals. And, worst of all, they allowed undesirables into their fellowship as full members: commoners, foreigners, slaves, and can you believe it, even women!

So ground the gossip mills of ancient Rome.

And there was an element of truth in each charge, even the allegation of cannibalism. Christians did "eat the body and drink the blood" of Christ in their celebration of the Lord's Supper, but of course not in the way the wagging tongues of Roman spies and rumormongers described.

Tertullian knew the ancient faith would prevail. He knew these wild innovations of human equality would overcome the ancient prejudices sooner or later. As early as the year A.D. 197 he could write: *We are but of yesterday, and we have filled every place among you—cities, islands, fortresses, towns, marketplaces, the very camps, tribes, companies, Senate, and Forum. We have left you only the (pagan) temples.*[136]

Early Christianity gave women equal status in the fellowship, an act almost unprecedented in world history. Even Paul, who admonishes women to follow social conventions and not disturb Roman cultural standards, promotes the ministry of women and heaps praise on the husband-and-wife team of Aquila and Priscilla, two early teachers of the faith. (Romans 16:3-5, Acts 18:1-3, and II Timothy 4:19 relate comments of the ancient Christian community about the pair.)

Yet, the Church quickly lost its frontrunner status in the cause of equal rights for men and women. The medieval church, following the poor example of Augustine, shunned women as leaders in the congregation of the Lord. Once condemned for its ground-breaking role in the equality of men and women, the medieval church settled back into comfortable old patterns of male supremacy once more. It was as though the wild, other-worldly theologies of extremist cults, like the gnostic faction which produced the Gospel of Thomas, had prevailed. In that pseudo-gospel we are told that women are so evil that they may inherit eternal life only by becoming a man! Other gnostic thinkers would say that matter is so totally evil that Jesus could not have been born of woman, He only appeared to be. Although the general character of the gnostic heresies was toward full emancipation of women—as was the teaching of Jesus—the church seized on the worst elements of gnostic docetism and dualism and let fall away the few good theological notions gnosticism had about the equality of the sexes.

But Truth has a way of bobbing to the surface every time it is submerged in a sea of falsehood. If Christian thinkers had followed the example of Jesus—who treated women as intellectual and spiritual equals—perhaps we would have been spared many centuries of men dominating the other half of the human race to our collective impoverishment.

Early in the development of modern mystical Christianity—the New Thought Christianity of the Christian sciences—women emerged as powerful leaders, pioneer thinkers, and doers. You would not be reading Unity publications today if not for the healing experience of a remarkable woman, Myrtle Fillmore.

In this study we shall briefly survey the contribution of three women prophets of modern mystical Christianity. Two founded movements which survive today. One taught

more teachers than any other early thinker in
the New Thought Christian era. All wrote,
taught, and lived their faith. If they had not
done what they did when they did, it is quite
probable that there would be no metaphysical
Christian movement in this century to carry
on the work of Christian mystics throughout
the ages.

They are Mary Baker Eddy, Emma Curtis
Hopkins, and Nona Brooks. Tides of history
brought these three women in sequential relationship to each other, as in the ancient world
where Socrates taught Plato, Plato taught
Aristotle, and Aristotle taught Alexander
the Great. No clear line such as this can be
found linking the three, but a linkage of relationships does exist. To explore who they
were and what they said, we must go back to
the days of the mid-nineteenth century once
more.

Emerson is still writing and lecturing at
Concord, although his health is beginnning to
fail. German absolute idealism of Kant and
Hegel has arrived in America as transcendentalism, advocated by Emerson, Parker, and a
bevy of other teachers. Mental healers, pat-
terned after the bizarre Frenchman Anton
Mesmer (1734-1815), travel the country giv-

ing various kinds of healings. They lay on hands, dispense medicine oils, and sometimes sell charms and talismen. Most are fakers and opportunists.

But in this crowd of charlatans there is one man who seems to have found a way to take the theories of Emerson and the transcendentalists and make them work in the realm of healing. His name is Phineas P. Quimby. Son of a blacksmith, Quimby spent most of his life in New England and died in 1866 at the age of sixty-three. Quimby believed he had rediscovered the healing secrets of Jesus. He started life as a "mesmerist" but moved to a practice of true spiritual/mental healing.

One of Quimby's patients was a woman named Mary Patterson. She had come to him with a long history of invalidism. Her husband, Dr. Patterson, wrote to Quimby at Portland, Maine, asking for his help. This excerpt is dated October 14, 1861: *My wife has been an invalid for a number of years; is not able to sit up but a little, and we wish to have the benefit of your wonderful power in her case. If you are soon coming to Concord I shall carry her up to you, and if you are not coming there we may try to carry her to Portland if you remain there.*

*Please write me at your earliest conve-
nience and oblige. Yours truly, Dr. D. Patterson, Rumney, N.H.*[137]

This brief letter, reproduced in "The Quimby Manuscripts" by Julius Dresser, an-
nounces the beginning of a new era in
American Protestantism. Mary Patterson
went to Portland and was eventually healed
by Dr. Quimby. She would later teach his
method to millions who came to know her by
the name Mary Baker Eddy.

Christian Science differs from New
Thought Christianity on several major theo-
logical/practical issues. For a detailed study
of these contrasting theologies, see Charles S.
Braden's book "Spirits in Rebellion: The Rise
and Development of New Thought" (Southern Methodist Press, 1980). Perhaps the
major difference between the two metaphysical movements is that Christian Science
denies the reality of matter, while New
Thought Christianity in general, and Unity in
particular, believes the world is real but can
be transcended by the spiritual element in the
human being.

There are, however, more similarities than
differences between Christian Science and
the rest of the modern mystical churches. The

opening words of Mary Baker Eddy's greatest work, "Science and Health," testifies to this commonality: *The prayer that reforms the sinner and heals the sick is an absolute faith that all things are possible to God, . . . a spiritual understanding of Him, an unselfed love.*[138]

Early in the development of New Thought, the term *Christian Science* was a generic one. Even the founders of Unity, Charles and Myrtle Fillmore, called their teachings Christian Science in the embryonic days of their movement. The term was abandoned by the Fillmores and other New Thought Christian pioneers chiefly because of Mrs. Eddy's repeated insistence that she alone had the right to use the label.[139]

Mrs. Eddy discovered that the Quimby method of healing by mental/spiritual means worked so well that she could teach others to employ it, too. Disease was error; Truth would overcome the false beliefs which caused the apparent sickness and misery. Therefore, she writes in "Science and Health:" . . . *The only reality of sin, sickness, or death is the awful fact that unrealities seem real to human erring belief, until God strips off their disguise. They are not true, because they are not of God.*[140]

There is a fierce controversy still raging as to whether Mrs. Eddy "learned" her method of healing from Quimby or "discovered" it herself. Her early writings are full of praise for Quimby. But later, as she became the center of a rapidly growing movement, she tried to put distance between herself and the other New Thought teachers by claiming that she owed her method to no one but God. Mrs. Eddy attacked in writing some of the other leaders, who often replied in kind. The situation was not very pleasant, and today the rift between mystical Christian churches like Unity and the Christian Science movement can be traced to those early, unresolved conflicts.

It is not within the scope of this article to solve so complex an issue as this. Let it suffice to say that Mrs. Eddy did go to Quimby and was healed afterward, that she taught a method similar to Quimby's discovery, and that she, more than any other person, was responsible for popularizing the mental/spiritual healing techniques now widely used by New Thought Christianity. If it were not for Mary Baker Eddy, we would probably not have any metaphysical Christian churches today.

One reason for this dependence on Mrs. Eddy as a founder of modern Christian mysticism is that she was responsible for introducing these ideas to another remarkable woman, our second prophet, Emma Curtis Hopkins. The importance of Emma Curtis Hopkins lies in the fact that she was, in the words of Braden, a "teacher's teacher." He writes: *The list of persons who sat under her teaching, either in Chicago ... or in some of the other cities where she taught ... reads like a Who's Who among New Thought leaders. To name only a few, there were Frances Lord, Annie Rix Militz, and Harriet Rix; Malinda E. Cramer, co-founder of Divine Science; Mrs. Bingham, teacher of Nona Brooks; Helen Williams; Charles and Myrtle Fillmore ... Dr. H. Emilie Cady ... Ella Wheeler Wilcox ... Elizabeth Towne; and considerably later Ernest Holmes, founder of the Church of Religious Science.*[141]

Imagine having that bunch over for tea! That's quite a list.

Mrs. Hopkins came to Mary Baker Eddy in 1883, and by September 1884 she was editor of "Christian Science Journal."[142] She and Mrs. Eddy had a disagreement over something; the subject is not known conclusively, although one historian claims it was because Mrs. Hopkins began to read other metaphysical books besides the works of Mary Baker Eddy.[143]

Emma Curtis Hopkins was a well-read, scholarly teacher. We hear echoes of Emerson and Parker in her writings: *Your idea of God must not be burdened with the transient and unreliable.*[144] And again: *Write the highest ideas of Good you have. You cannot write a stroke higher than the slave's idea of Good, but you will find that such a practice will pin you down to the truth, and it is in Truth that there is power. All the sacred books of the earth tell that God is Truth, and that Truth is God.*[145]

She taught the basic New Thought concepts of affirmation and denial, although she went along with Mary Baker Eddy in that matter had no reality since all is spirit.

Emma Curtis Hopkins founded no lasting movement of her own, but her students went forth to change their world. One of those pupils was a woman known to history only as Mrs. Bingham. She suffered from a malady which took her from her husband and children in Pueblo, Colorado, to seek a specialist in Chicago in the 1880s.

The doctor told Mrs. Bingham he could help her only if she stayed in Chicago for a year of treatment. Dismayed and desperate, lonely for her family, Mrs. Bingham was advised by a friend to seek Emma Curtis Hopkins. She did and was healed. She returned home to Pueblo and began classes, teaching the techniques she learned from Mrs. Hopkins. Mrs. Bingham invited the Brooks sisters, Alethea and Nona, to attend those classes. Good Presbyterians, they refused the invitation. Mrs. Bingham knew the two women were not well. Nona could eat only a few soft foods without terrible pain in her throat. The new teacher changer her tactics. The dialogue exchange between the sisters and their self-appointed teacher is recorded in the biography of Nona Brooks, "Powerful Is the Light": *"This time I am not inviting you,"* Mrs. Bingham stated, fixing Alethea with her eye. *"I am commanding you. I will not take 'no' for an answer."*

After Mrs. Bingham left, Nona cried out, "But Sister, you didn't promise her? We simply can't do it!"[146]

But she had promised, and so the proper young Presbyterians scuttled off to a class in

metaphysical healing. Soon they were working on affirmations and denials, and soon
after that, Nona was healed in a miraculous,
light-filled experience.

I visited the mother church of Divine
Science in Denver and talked with some of
the members who had known Nona Brooks.
They were unanimous in their memories of
her as a warm, gentle human being with a
strength that came from conviction. I heard
the word "motherly" again and again. I met
Mary Lou Benn who was christened and married by Miss Brooks, spoke with her secretary and others who knew her simply as their
pastor.

Frances Marsh knew Nona Brooks inti-
mately; she was her secretary. A tiny lady
with sparkling eyes and a quick wit, Mrs.
Marsh told me that Nona Brooks was a
strong but humble woman with a sweet
chuckle that went with her good sense of
humor. They would sit in the kitchen of First
Divine Science Church in Denver, telling
stories and enjoying the fellowship of mystical Christians. The gathering place for Nona
Brooks' staff in unofficial meetings was a
large kitchen worktable with a massive wood
top, around which they sat on stools.

Mrs. Marsh recalls Nona Brooks saying that she always remembered to thank God for her sense of humor, her "funnybone," she called it.

Reverend Marjorie James told me a story about a young woman who worked at the Denver Zoological Gardens and faced a transfer to the reptile section. Terrified of snakes, she asked Miss Brooks to go along with her on her first day, not knowing that serpents struck terror in the heart of the great Nona Brooks, too. But Miss Brooks reasoned that if God truly is everywhere, He must be with the snakes, too.

After fervent prayer, she went with the young woman. They fed the reptiles without incident. That, I thought as I listened to Reverend James, is truly *practical* Christianity in action.

If there were a central creed of New Thought Christianity—which there is not and hopefully never will be—perhaps it would be the belief that there is only one Power and one Presence in our lives and in the universe, God, the good omnipotent. This describes the fountainhead of all that Nona Brooks taught. In "Powerful Is the Light," Hazel Deane records another dialogue exchange which

summarizes Nona Brooks' teaching on one
Power/one Presence. Someone said: *"Mortal
mind gets us into trouble and Immortal Mind
gets us out."*

*"But if you want to get well you have to
stay your attention on the immortal, the
perfect," said Nona soberly. "You'll never get
well by thinking imperfection. Perfect God
and perfect man, that is the basis. Not mortal
mind and Immortal Mind! Not two but One,
and that one, God. Perfect! Everywhere present! Not two minds, but One, One, One."*[147]

There are so many echoes of great Christian thinkers we have studied before in this
quote that we cannot spend the time in this
brief survey to make the connections called
for in an in-depth analysis. Briefly, we hear
Hegel's assertion that the essence of reality
is oneness, not duality, and that even good
and evil are really two ends of one process.
We hear Emerson's insistence on the perfectability of the human soul, George Fox's cry
for "openings" through the Inner Light, and
Meister Eckehart's preaching that man and
God are one. In fact, the movement (known
variously as Divine Science, Religious
Science, and Unity) of modern mystical
Christianity stands in a long line of great

thinkers—orthodox and unorthodox—who have continually taught that God and man are Father and Child, one Power and Presence pervading all that is.

In our final two studies we shall see that these ideas have spilled over into the most orthodox of modern theological circles. We shall look at two of the greatest theologians of the twentieth century, one Protestant and one Catholic. In the writings and teachings of Dr. Paul Tillich and Father Pierre Teilhard de Chardin we shall find ideas which Christian theology today considers revolutionary, epoch-making, futuristic. There is a strange similarity between what these two intellectual giants have said and the teachings of three women prophets of mystical Christianity: Mary Baker Eddy, Emma Curtis Hopkins, and Nona Brooks.

Tillich and Chardin are probably the most important thinkers we shall study because their ideas are today influencing Christian thought worldwide. I have a fantasy that shows a host of mystical Christians who have gone to the next world, standing on a cloud (pardon the conventionality, but it's *my* fantasy) and looking down at these "new" ideas with undisguised delight. Meister

Eckehart turns to Nona Brooks and says, "Well, Sister, it's about time, ja?"

Maybe the title of this series came from that fantasy. From the direction that modern theology is taking, it appears we do have lots of friends in high places. Ja?

11

Shaking the Foundations
Dr. Paul Tillich
(1886-1965)

To understand the contribution of Paul
Tillich to modern Christian theology we must
take a quick look at twentieth-century religious thinkers leading up to him, especially
his contemporaries in the "neoorthodox"
school. That label need not frighten those of
us in the liberal schools of Protestantism.
Neoorthodoxy was a reaction against the late
nineteenth-century theologies which placed
undue emphasis on "natural" religion.

With the Enlightenment, modern humanity has wondered about the origins of its religious ideas. In the Middle Ages no one dared

question the authority of generally held Christian truth: the Church said it, they believed it, and that settled it. But expansion of European Christianity both eastward—where they encountered a highly advanced Islamic civilization—and westward—where a New World beckoned with temptations to independent thought—brought long-suppressed doubts and questions to the surface at last. Long overdue, skepticism at first was good medicine for everyone. Doubt became outright disbelief, however, in the heyday of European philosophy of the nineteenth century. Wildly radical thinkers like Karl Marx decided that God was a drug brewed up by the priestly caste in collaboration with rich overlords for the purpose of keeping the masses in line.

Within Christian thought the battle lines were drawn along a front between those who believed humanity had taught itself about God by what it could learn in the world, so-called "natural theology," and those who believed God had reached down to us in a special revelation of His nature and purposes. This latter group became known as the neo-orthodox school because it took the revelation of God in Christ as given by the Scriptures seriously (hence *orthodoxly*) and yet made good use of modern biblical scholarship in point to the human element in the writing of the biblical materials (hence *neo* or new).

Karl Barth (pronounced *Bart*) provoked the modern controversy which is still raging in the theological circles when he published his "Commentary on the Epistle to the Romans" in 1919. Written in the war-weary days of World War I, his commentary said that human sciences could not solve all our problems, that we needed the special revelation of God as shown in the nature and person of Jesus Christ. To a Christendom which had seen its sons die by poison gases or mowed down by machine-gun fire across no-man's-land, the message rang like a bell at midnight.

Rudolf Bultmann was the second German-speaking theologian to powerfully influence twentieth-century Christian thought. Bultmann pointed out correctly that the Bible is written in prescientific language by people who believed the Earth was flat, heaven was in the clouds above their heads, and hell was inside the Earth below their feet. We do not have to accept the three-story universe of ancient thought to see there is eternal truth contained within our Scriptures. One can hear echoes of Origen and other people we have studied in these comments by Bultmann. Dr. Bultmann was one of the foremost biblical scholars of this century, too. He embarked on a program of sifting through the New Testament to cull from it the eternal truths, the *kerygma*, which are there. He called this process *demythologizing*. It is the work of all biblical scholarship even to this day.

Bultmann and Barth were contemporaries of Tillich. Barth, in fact, was an exact contemporary since they were both born in 1886. Tillich came to the United States in 1933 after he was fired from his teaching post for outspoken criticism of the Nazis.

Tillich was both a theologian and a philosopher. Hence, his work appealed to a broad range of people and was therefore criticized from both sides by his opponents. His field of philosophy is called *ontology*, or the study of existence. The older name for ontology is metaphysics, although Tillich avoided that term because metaphysical speculation was unpopular among professional philosophers during his lifetime. Ontology was acceptable, but metaphysics was not. Strange breed, those philosophers.

Karl Barth had insisted that human life must be understood only in terms of God's revelation to us. That meant that even the questions we seek to answer must come from God's activity, not our own curiosity. Tillich rejected this extreme, arguing that natural theology has a place in that everyday experience provides us with problems to overcome, eternal questions of all the religions of humanity: Why is there evil? What must I do to experience renewal? How can I overcome my limitations and be what I am intended to be? How can I get along with my neighbor, my family, my associates? What is a good person, and how do I become one?

These kinds of questions arise from our human, everyday existence. Hence they are *existential.* We cannot go to the Scriptures empty, expecting to find questions and answers like some divine catechism. We do our religious thinking as flesh-and-blood people living in real circumstances. Religion must speak to everyday life and provide answers to our deepest questions, not just idly speculate on fine points of dogma. Tillich writes: *No myth, no mystical vision, no metaphysical principle, no sacred law, has the concreteness of a personal life. In comparison with a personal life everything else is relatively abstract.*[148]

And that is exactly what we have in the Christian faith—eternal Truth revealed within the everyday experiences of a personal life, the life of Jesus Christ. Thus, Tillich builds a bridge between natural and revealed theology, between those who say God can be discovered in the world and those who insist that only God can let Himself be known. To this Tillich replies that God has let Himself be known, and we can know Him through Jesus the Christ, *because* we are in the world that Jesus knew.

Tillich's system sets forth a method of correlation between natural and revealed religion. We look to human experience for the problems and questions, to the divine revelation in Christ for the answers. A contemporary of Tillich, the great New York preacher Harry Emerson Fosdick, used a similar method from his world-famous pulpit at Riverside Baptist Church. Fosdick said a preacher should speak his message with the newspaper in one hand (existential situation) and the Bible in the other (divine truth).

Armed with Bultmann's notions of a demythologized Scripture, Tillich set forth to correlate the problems of twentieth-century society with the answers found in the kerygma, that kernel of Truth within the pages of holy Scripture. This is no mindless biblical fundamentalism but a sophisticated system of looking at the real problems of everyday life and matching them to the answers implicit in the New Testament. It allows for some mighty interesting deductions, especially when Tillich the philosopher is talking. We shall consider the main points in his theology/philosophy in the briefest ways. These seem to be Tillich's doctrine of God and his teaching on symbolism. Soon the echoes of other mystical/metaphysical thinkers we have studied will begin to thunder in our ears as we see how closely what Unity teaches in its deepest theological insights parallels the thinking of Paul Tillich.

Doctrine of God: the Ground of Our Being

Dr. Tillich waded into the deepest question of all: what is God like? Is God a Supreme Being, an infinite chief executive with His office somewhere beyond the heavens or in some other spiritual dimension? Does that make

God just another being among all the lesser beings that exist? Is God "personal"? Does God have moods, feelings, bad days? Does God play favorites? If the answers to these questions are not forthcoming, what can we say about God that is true?

Tillich correlated these questions with the insights of modern biblical scholarship and modern existential philosophy. His answers are astounding. Dr. Paul Tillich, the leading Protestant theologian of this century, declared that God does not exist. Now, before we write him off as another disciple of Marx and the wild-eyed radicals, we need to note that Paul Tillich deeply believed in God. He just didn't believe God *exists* like we exist. Let's take an example from everyday life.

A chair has qualities to it—hardness or softness, brownness or blackness, woody scent or odor of plastic. It possesses these attributes which describe what it is. But it also has another quality about it that we take for granted: it exists. It doesn't have to exist, but it does. It possesses the power of existence.

Everything we know in the world also has this power of existence, this power to be. The room you are in right now has walls, a floor, a ceiling. There are probably chairs, electrical appliances, and things hanging on the walls. None of these things has to exist. There is no reason why the chair you are sitting in has to be, but it is.

This equation carries over into the cosmos. There is no reason for anything to be. In fact, an empty universe—darkness without light, energy, or matter—would be more "natural." Yet, there are stars, galaxies of them swirling in inexorable orbits with teeming trillions of worlds where life probably has evolved. All of this is very nice, but unnecessary.

Science is an attempt to understand what is.

Ontology—we call it metaphysics—goes beyond physical sciences and dares to ask the question, "Why?" Why is there something instead of nothing? Why is there goodness and love in a universe supposedly forever grinding on its mindless axis? What is the power to be that manifests itself as matter, energy, and thought?

Paul Tillich leaped boldly to a conclusion. God does not "exist," he said, because *God is existence.* God is the very power to be. He called it the "ground of our being."

In his own words: *The being of God is*

being-itself. The being of God cannot be understood as the existence of a being alongside others or above others. If God is a being, he is subject to the categories of finitude, especially to space and substance. Even if he is called the "highest being" in the sense of the "most perfect" and the "most powerful" being, this situation is not changed. When applied to God, superlatives become diminutives . . . . Many confusions in the doctrine of God and many apologetic weaknesses could be avoided if God were understood first of all as being-itself or as the ground of being. The power of being . . . .[149]

Tillich is not the easiest theologian to read, but when you take him seriously and slowly you find that his sentences are jam-packed with marvelous insights. Some authors give the impression of a tap dancer trying to keep the audience entertained while the stage crew puts out the fire backstage. Tillich reads more like a crib-sheet for an exam about the nature of reality.

Along with the notion that God is not a being must stand the doctrine, widely held in Unity circles, that God is therefore not personal but impersonal. Dr. H. Emilie Cady writes in what is perhaps the best-known

Unity book, *Lessons in Truth: Many have thought of God as a personal being. The statement that God is Principle chills them, and in terror they cry out, "They have taken away my Lord, and I know not where they have laid him." (John 20:13)*

Broader and more learned minds are always cramped by the thought of God as a person, for personality limits to place and time.

God is the name we give to that unchangeable, inexorable principle at the source of all existence. [150]

What better description of God as the ground of our being could there be? Tillich did not mean that God is uncaring, unloving, unfeeling. He meant that God as being itself encompasses all there is, to include these personal attributes. The problem with our understanding of God has come from our lack of familiarity with the nature of symbolism.

Teaching on Symbolism

Some New Thought Christians see all external symbols as dangerous traps, luring people away from the contemplation of Christ within. All traditional "church trappings" are regarded as signs of lower levels of spirituality—stained-glass windows, crosses, use of bread and wine for communion, water for christening or baptism. But what always happens when we eliminate a series of symbols is that another set pops up to fill the need: meditation rooms, flower communions, and so on.

In fact, humans are irrevocably symbolic. We write poetry to talk about spring or winter. We draw pictures and take photographs. We use visual aids like slides, overhead projectors, movies. We listen to music, which is a symbolic representation of feelings and mood.

With our religious thought, symbolism becomes more prevalent. How can we talk of infinity, omnipresence, and omnipotence unless we use symbolic language? Describe infinity. Paint a picture of omnipresence. Give a demonstration of omnipotence.

It can be done, but only with symbols. Perhaps that's why Jesus spoke in parables when He taught. He must have realized that there is no way finite humans can comprehend God totally. The question is not, "Shall we worship the true God or an idol?" The question is, "Which idol shall we worship?" Which word-picture of the utterly inexplicable shall we paint? Jesus saw that our God-concept is symbolic, and must be, and so He spoke and acted symbolically.

Dr. Tillich made some profound observations about the nature of symbolism as it is related to Christian theology. He writes in "Systematic Theology": *There can be no doubt that any concrete assertion about God must be symbolic, for a concrete assertion is one which uses a segment of finite experience in order to say something about him.*[151]

Great religious symbols grow from the rich life-experiences of a people of faith. They cannot be manufactured by a community of scholars unless the worshiping community finds the symbol meets its needs to express something about the divine.

The best example I can think of to "symbolize" this is my experience with Army helicopters in Vietnam. I was a medical evacuation pilot. I flew an aircraft officially designated by the name *Iroquois*. We flew into hot spots accompanied by another helicopter called a *Cayuse*. Sometimes high-ranking officers would observe our rescue mission from a third aircraft, officially named a *Kiowa*.

No one called the helicopters *Iroquois*,

Cayuse, or *Kiowa.* They were, respectively: *Hueys, Loaches,* and *Rangers.* These nicknames took the place of the official word-symbols for the helicopters so completely that if you are a Vietnam veteran you may have flown in one of them without ever knowing its proper name.

A symbol does more than point to another reality beyond itself. A good symbol, Tillich said, participates in the reality it is symbolizing. The cross, for example, is more than a symbol of Christianity; it is an integral part of the Christian faith. The cross is a symbol of the one Power and Presence of God—the horizontal bar representing God's omnipresence, the vertical bar showing God's power flowing downward to humanity. It is also a symbol of perseverance in suffering, and God's willingness to forgive us for stumbling on the path.

Yet, for hundreds of years the cross was a symbol of terror and death. Not until Constantine's time did the cross become a widely used symbol for the faith, because in the early centuries of the Christian era, people were still being crucified.

The problem with symbols is that they are so powerful. If a symbol becomes so powerful in the minds of people, it can literally take over and eclipse that which it is trying to symbolize. The Bible can become God's handwritten document, instead of a symbolic retelling of the good news. The statue of a saint can become the saint in the minds of the people.

There is an Eastern parable which says that if you meet the Buddha on the road to your spiritual enlightenment, you must kill him. This cryptic saying means that even a teacher as great as Buddha can become a hindrance if we rely on him too much, if he becomes our goal instead of God-consciousness.

That is why Tillich insists that we must continue to think of God as personal, even though we know that God utterly transcends the limitations of personality, finitude, and being: *The symbol "personal God" is absolutely fundamental because an existential relationship is person-to-person. Man cannot be ultimately concerned about anything that is less than personal....*[152]

Hence we needed a good symbol for God that was personal, existential (everyday), and hinted at divinity. The greatest symbol for God is, Tillich contends, Jesus Christ. Jesus is what Harvard Professor Gordon Kaufman calls the "focused God"—the place we choose to go to see what divinity is like. When we do that, we must do it with full awareness of the dangers implicit in symbolism, dangers which some New Thought Christians have rightly pointed out in the past.

To be symbol-free, however, is both impossible and undesirable. What we need, Dr. Tillich contends, is a better understanding of the ancient symbols for a modern age. Most of us automatically translate the "up" and "down" language of the Bible and our old hymns into spiritual terms. However, when the biblical writers recorded and edited their accounts, they took that up-and-down talk seriously. Heaven was up in the clouds, and the land of the dead was down under the earth, as Bultmann has pointed out. Tillich contends that we need to do the same for symbols like *God*, translating the old notion of a Supreme Being into thought-pictures of God as Existence itself, the very power to be, the ground of our being. Loving principle. Caring law. Ultimately concerned energy-process of which we are all part.

Even such traditional ideas as bread and wine for communion could be recovered as a

New Thought Christian practice under Tillich's concept of symbolism, for what better symbolism could there be for uniting the God-in-the-world with the God-in-me than partaking of Holy Communion? And if we truly believe God is everywhere, He is surely in the bread and wine as well.

All symbolism would have to speak authentically to the needs of a worshiping community, and so no church agency could enforce any practices or rituals or symbols upon its people with any lasting success under Tillich's concepts. The test of a symbol will continue to be the test of time.

Paul Tillich's sermons have been collected in books titled "Shaking of the Foundations," "The New Being," and "The Eternal Now."[153] His interpreters are legion, perhaps the most famous and most controversial of whom is Bishop John A. T. Robinson. Bishop Robinson published a powerful little book in 1963 titled "Honest to God," which shook the Christian world in general and his own Anglican Church in particular with its Tillichian proclamations. It is highly readable and can be disturbing in the questions it asks, but it is pure Tillich.[154]

Paul Tillich was in many ways another

bridge builder like Emerson and Parker. He wanted to find in the ancient faith answers to the questions of today. He saw a grand unity of things, a simple yet magnificent vision of God as the power to be, the ground of our being. His writings are still required reading for most students in virtually every mainline theological seminary. His vision of God is none other than the biblical picture of God as the one Power and Presence, taught by New Thought Christianity for nearly a century.

Paul Tillich—anti-Nazi activist, seminary professor, ontological philosopher, and perhaps the most read and respected Protestant theologian of the twentieth century—said and taught a lot of things that sound very familiar to students of metaphysical Christianity.

In our final study we look at a controversial Catholic theologian whose works were banned until after his death. Pierre Teilhard de Chardin stands in a class by himself among orthodox religious thinkers. However, he does not stand alone in modern Christianity, as we shall see in the last chapter of this work. Like Tillich, Teilhard de Chardin provokes debate and dissent because his ideas are beyond the ken of regular theology. Yet it may be this obscure mystical Jesuit whom theological writers of the future will cite as the turning point in orthodoxy, the man who brought together science and mysticism for the edification and spiritual growth of generations yet unborn.

12

Faith for the Future
Teilhard de Chardin
(1881-1955)

*And he who sat upon the throne said,
"Behold, I make all things new." Also he
said, "Write this, for these words are trust-
worthy and true." And he said to me, "It is
done! I am the Alpha and the Omega, the beginning and the end. To the thirsty I will give
from the fountain of the water of life without
payment. He who conquers shall have this
heritage, and I will be his God and he shall be
my son."* (Rev. 21:5-7)[155]

We come to the end of our series in which
we have investigated the many "friends"

Unity has in the great sweep of Christian history. We have found that modern metaphysical Christianity is an important branch of the great family tree of the ancient faith. The only walls separating us from our brothers and sisters in other Christian churches are the walls of prejudice and misunderstanding.

We are a part of Christian heritage, history, and theology, as these studies have clearly shown. We are also on the cutting edge of exciting new ideas which are today dominating Christian thought and teaching in virtually every mainline seminary in the Western world.

Mystical Christianity is not just an integral part of the past and present. It speaks as the faith for the future. We can see this clearly when we look at where Christian thought seems to be headed. Our last study is dedicated to this.

There looms on the horizon of Christian theology a recently discovered giant. A man has walked among us whose views on the nature of life, God, and the future are so profound that some scholars believe it will take five hundred years for humanity to understand and integrate into daily life the ideas taught by this great new prophet.

He was not a herald of some radical new sect. He was no pseudo-mystic, peddling his books and offering seminars to hosts of his novices for a price.

He was a Jesuit priest named Pierre Teilhard de Chardin.

Teilhard (pronounced "tay-ar") published nothing during his lifetime except through informal dissemination of his ideas in mimeograph form. His works were banned by the Jesuits and frowned upon by the great lords of the Catholic hierarchy. Today that church not only has lifted the ban but has displayed a measure of embarrassment that bureaucrats once tried to silence the greatest Catholic thinker of modern times.

As has been said of him: *The Society of Jesus* (Jesuit order) *refused... publication and refused him permission to teach philosophy or be a candidate for a professorship. As late as June 30, 1962, seven years after his death, the Vatican issued a warning in which bishops, religious superiors, and rectors of clerical training were urged "to protect minds, especially young minds, against the dangers of the works of Father Teilhard de Chardin and his supporters.*[156]

A man of great spiritual insight, Teilhard blessed and released these misguided zealots. Writer T. A. Kantonen says that Teilhard prayed he would not die bitter. A selection from his book "The Divine Milieu" suggests he was successful: *Throughout my life, by means of my life, the world has little by little caught fire in my sight until, aflame all around me, it has become almost completely luminous from within. . . . Such has been my experience in contact with the earth—the diaphany of the Divine at the heart of the universe on fire . . . Christ; his heart; a fire: capable of penetrating everywhere and, gradually, spreading everywhere.*[157]

To understand Teilhard, one must have a good background in the sciences of anthropology, biology, genetics, geology, paleontology, physics, and zoology. Because much of his work is technical, we shall look at the conclusions he drew and try to keep the scientific data in simple, summary form. We must dip into the sciences in this study because Teilhard was a thinker who worked as a research scientist in the field of *paleontology*, the study of the fossil record, and who specialized in the origin and prehistory of the human race.

What he set out to do was to provide a bridge between scientific knowledge and mystical Christianity, to show for all time that Truth is one. It was a task somewhat like that which Charles Fillmore took upon himself. The advantage Teilhard had was living later in the twentieth century than Charles Fillmore. He was heir to much better scientific information and an excellent university education, as well as lifelong field work as a practicing scientist. Fillmore's accomplishment was all the more extraordinary because of his educational limitations.

Teilhard de Chardin's handicap was formal education. He found he had to rethink everything he had been taught about the "Phenomenon of Man," which is the title of his magnum opus. Scientific exploration was explained to him in purely materialistic terms. Random factors interacting upon themselves produced random results, moving along a random course toward a random destination. To Teilhard, this made scientists no more than glorified accident investigators. Moreover, it left unanswered some of the most fundamental questions about the nature of human experience.

First, if everything is randomly proceeding,

why is it that we can chart the progress? Why does nature seem to select smarter, healthier species over less intelligent, weaker ones? The fossil record shows an onward-and-upward march from the primeval slime to us high-tech denizens dwelling on the edge of the twenty-first century.

Life came forth from nonlife. But it didn't stop there. It continued to progress until creatures evolved who could think. Are we to assume that this is an accident, when a long line of events lead in a logical sequence to a conclusion?

Furthermore, are we to assume that this is the end of the evolutionary line? Is there a stage of existence beyond our present level of consciousness? In other words, where are we headed? Any rudimentary study of the ages of the earth will show the great sweep of evolution. How can we say, therefore, that all this order and symmetry is accidental?

Teilhard set out to integrate his spiritual insights with his scientific knowledge. The results are not always coherent, and we may not agree with all the elements in his conclusions. However, the similarities between the theories of this scientist-priest and the teachings of mystical Christians like Charles

Fillmore are astounding. As we look to these parallels, we must remember that Teilhard is considered by many orthodox scholars to be the thinker of the future, the one upon whom vast superstructures of theological teaching will be based for perhaps centuries to come. One scholar writes: *It is necessary to be Teilhardian because if evolution is as important and is to be described as Teilhard describes it, then certain theological positions which have been very carefully elaborated by Latin theology, and notably anthropology, will very soon be destitute of all meaning. Or, what amounts to the same thing, they will belong to the prehistory of theological thought.*[158]

Perhaps the first Unity publication to take notice of the importance of Teilhard to mystical Christianity was Marcus Bach's *The Unity Way*. Bach, a United Church of Christ minister and religious scholar of wide repute, compares Charles Fillmore's *Atom-Smashing Power of Mind* with Teilhard's great work, "Phenomenon of Man": *Teilhard . . . was speaking in scientific terms, in theological terms, in evolutionary terms of the identical theme that Charles Fillmore had presented in the sweep and spirit of inspired metaphysics .... Someday someone will do a comparative scholarly study of these two books and these two men and show how Fillmore saw unity as being the nature of things, and how Teilhard viewed the nature of things as being in unity.*[159]

That challenge must await a more lengthy treatment than we can allow in a single chapter. But if the predictions of Teilhard's lasting significance prove correct, sooner or later the academic world and its theological scholars must notice that Fillmore, self-educated mystic though he was, anticipated the discoveries proclaimed by scientist-priest Pierre Teilhard de Chardin. In fact, I venture a prediction: There will come a day when three thinkers will stand out as beacon lights of our age: Ralph Waldo Emerson, whom Marcus Bach calls the "Father of New Thought," Teilhard de Chardin, and Charles Fillmore. Bach seems to agree: *It is in these books that Fillmore also reveals his inseparable kinship with Emerson. It is here that the father of Unity* (Fillmore) *and the father of New Thought* (Emerson) *would both receive the blessing of Teilhard de Chardin. For Fillmore and Emerson in probing the phenomenon of man discover the phenomenon of*

God . . . here that modern metaphysics is challenged to keep step with science and with the unlimited activity of human thought.[160]

We may refine, rethink, rework their discoveries; we can never overlook them. Emerson gave literary and intellectual expression to these ideas; Fillmore intuitively wove a system of thought and action from the best popular science and philosophy of his day; Teilhard took the essence of mystical Christianity and expressed it in scientific language and symbolism. Some scientists of an earlier time tended to sneer at religious insights. A researcher as well-known as behavioral psychologist B. F. Skinner could write a best-selling book that proclaimed humanity has grown "Beyond Freedom and Dignity" and has no need for God.

With the publication and dissemination of Teilhard's works, the sneering stopped. Perhaps his vision is one which all humanity will share when this turbulent era boils down into values and mythologies that can be embraced by our whole society.

Teilhard takes us back to the beginning. Not the simple biblical beginning expressed in the prescientific language of the book of Genesis, but the primordial darkness before matter condensed from the energies of the "big bang" some fifteen billion years ago. Teilhard shows us how energy formed into matter, how matter became atoms, and atoms built up into molecules. Ever more complex, ever more diversified, these inorganic structures eventually evolved into primitive organic compounds from which the stuff of life is grown.

Organic compounds became simple one-cell creatures, which specialized and cooperated to form multicell creatures. From there it was onward and upward to thinking, rational beings like us.

This much causes no stir in the scientific world. Regardless what television evangelists may say over the airwaves in their attacks on evolution, this "theory" is so well-established today that to overthrow organic evolution we would have to throw out many of the scientific advances in genetics, geology, paleontology, microbiology, botany, and medicine accumulated over the last half century. A glance at the walls of the Grand Canyon gives us a printout of the evolutionary track record that should convince anyone with an open mind.

Millions of years ago, the landmass

through which the Colorado River flows became uplifted, causing the river to run much more swiftly. The result was that in a comparatively short period of geological time (millions of years instead of hundreds of millions), the Colorado River cut downward through its riverbed and gouged out the Grand Canyon.

Slicing through the Earth's crust, the river laid bare a fossil record that stretches back to the dawn of life. At the lowest levels, simple fossils can be found. As you ascend the walls of the canyon, more complex creatures are always appearing. There are no mammals down at the lowest levels, and no dinosaurs on the top. This view of the ages of the earth establishes that evolution occurred just as theorists said it did. Simpler creatures gave way to more complex; duller brains evolved into smarter ones. Everything moved upward toward its crowning achievement, a thinking person, homo sapiens. That's us.

Teilhard goes beyond the limits of ordinary science at this point, for he dares to ask why. Why did inorganic matter evolve into the primordial soup from which living things emerged? Why did more intelligent creatures supercede those with less brainpower? Why did the universe evolve creatures who could question their very existence? In other words, why did energy move to become matter, which moved to become thinking beings?

The answer he gave startled the scientific community, although it does not seem terribly revolutionary to those of us in the mystical Christian tradition. Teilhard said that evolution is not a random process: it knows where it's going. Life itself has within it a drive to produce better, healthier, smarter creatures. Why? Because the energy of life is being drawn toward something way off in the evolutionary distance. He called that destination the *Omega Point,* and identified it with Christ. We would call it "Christ consciousness."

To the process of evolution toward higher consciousness he gave a new name, *noogenesis* (From the Greek words *nous* meaning *mind* and *genesis* meaning *beginnings*). In fact, Teilhard's works are rich with new terms grown from his fertile mind.

He sees all consciousness as converging at some time in the distant future, the Omega Point. We must remind ourselves that he is speaking as neither a theologian nor a speculative philosopher, but as a research scientist of impeccable credentials. Teilhard says if we look at the trend of evolution we must conclude that higher consciousness is the ultimate goal since that is where nature has most heavily invested its energies. Teilhard even goes so far as to say it is love—the attraction of two elements and their union in relationship—which holds the atoms of the universe together.

T. A. Kantonen gives an excellent commentary on Teilhard's thought in his book "Christian Faith Today": *In Teilhard the passion of the religious man for a God to adore and the passion of the scientific thinker for a unifying principle of the universe are beautifully blended together. On the one hand, he can say, "What I cry out for, like every being, with my whole life and all my earthly passion is a God to adore." On the other hand, the whole panorama of cosmic evolution moving toward a more and more complex union and culminating in a union of love among men would be meaningless without a personal cosmic center and source of love, God.* [161]

In fact, life makes no sense unless something like the vision of Teilhard turns out to be true. Why would a mindless, inorganic evolutionary process move toward higher and higher levels of consciousness unless there were something about the very mechanism of reality which is consciousness itself? Did not another great twentieth-century thinker, Dr. Paul Tillich, say that God is the ground of our being, the very power to be?

In what direction does Teilhard see humanity going? It is here that the scientist becomes something of a mystic. He envisions a destiny beyond mere physical evolution for humankind. Kantonen describes Teilhard's eschatoloty: *The Omega Point is not in the converging lines themselves but out of this world altogether. Propelled by the love instilled in the cosmic "divine milieu" the unified multiple is moving toward a "critical threshold" where it will make one final leap forward out of the world to the Omega Point. In this ultimate sense human destiny lies outside this planet... And the Omega Point is Christ, the Alpha and the Omega, the first and the last, the beginning and the end. Christ, the radiant incarnation of divine love, not only permeates all reality and impels it toward its ultimate goal but he is also the culmination of the whole cosmic process.*[162]

In the creation of the universe we see

energy spreading out in all directions. Kantonen likens this to an impulse bursting forth from the South Pole in all directions northward. When this impulse reaches the equator, it will be at maximum distance from its source. It will then begin to reconverge toward the North Pole, which is the same source it emerged from at the South Pole. When these divergent impulses come together at the top of the world—which represents this critical threshold of Teilhard's thinking—love and fulfillment will catapult human consciousness beyond the converging lines to the Source itself. We will become one with God.

Yet, Teilhard insists, we shall still be individual entities. He shows that union differentiates, all through the march of evolutionary progress. When a one-cell creature joins up with others to form a multicell organism, some of the cells take over special functions like digestion, breathing, etc., which every cell had to do by itself. When people band together in towns, some people can build houses, while others grow crops, and others tend to animals. Union does not make things similar; it differentiates and gives each a chance to do what he can do best.

So in his vision of the ultimate destiny of humanity, Teilhard sees us as one with God but still ourselves. I shall be, so to speak, that piece of God which is me. You shall be that bit of God which is you, forever. When we achieve this, we shall leap beyond this world and take wings of spirit, forever to dwell creatively in union with the divine creativity, God.

Although Teilhard suggested no symbols to represent his vision of our ultimate destiny beyond the physical world, there is an ancient Egyptian logo which might fill the need quite well some day in the future. What better symbol for the leap of consciousness beyond this world into the Omega Point than a winged globe?

Teilhard prayed for the coming of this kingdom in his beautiful "Hymn of the Universe." Here is an excerpt: *Disperse, O Jesus, the clouds with your lightning! Show yourself to us as the Mighty, the Radiant, the Risen! . . . And so that we should triumph over the world with you, come to us clothed in the glory of the world.*[163]

Pierre Teilhard de Chardin stands at the door to tomorrow. But behind him in unbroken line stands our heritage in the ancient faith. Men like Philo Judaeus, who created metaphysical Bible interpretation in the first century A.D.; women like Emma Curtis Hopkins and Nona Brooks, pioneers of modern New Thought Christianity; scholars like John Scotus Erigena; mystics like Meister Eckehart and George Fox; great writers like Ralph Waldo Emerson, and outspoken social critics and activists like Theodore Parker; giants in Christian theology like Origen, Pelagius, Tillich, and Teilhard. Heretic and orthodox thinker, rebel, and churchman, scholar and enthusiast—the tapestry of Christianity is woven from the fabric of men and women such as these.

There are other people who also contributed to New Thought Christianity. We could have studied ancient thinkers like Plato, Proclus, Clement of Alexandria, or Theodore of Mopsuestia. Or we could have looked at medieval theologians like Thomas Aquinas, Francis of Assisi, Catherine of Sienna, Bernard of Clairvaux, or the unknown author of the "Cloud of Unknowing" or Thomas á Kempis, author of "The Imitation of Christ."

Then there are the multitudes of reformation era mystics and thinkers we could have summoned as witnesses for our metaphysical heritage: Jakob Böhme, William Law, St. Teresa of Avila, or even Martin Luther and Huldrych Zwingli.

Into the modern age, we could have studied Charles Wesley, William Ellery Channing, Hosea Ballou, Simone Weil, Thomas Merton, Albert Schweitzer, Mahatma Ghandi, or Dag Hammarskjöld. Of living thinkers we could refer to Marcus Bach, Hans Küng, Norman Vincent Peale, and many others.

But perhaps the finest summary of the movement of consciousness toward the Omega Point was written by Teilhard de Chardin in "Hymn of the Universe": *Receive, O Lord, this all-embracing host which your whole creation, moved by your magnetism, offers you at this dawn of a new day.*

This bread, our toil, is of itself, I know, but an immense fragmentation; this wine, our pain, is no more, I know, than a draught that dissolves. Yet in the very depths of this formless mass you have implanted—and this I am sure of, for I sense it—a desire, irresistible, hallowing, which makes us cry out, believer and unbeliever alike: "Lord, make us one."[164]

Yesterday, today, and tomorrow we have friends in high places. Of this heritage we can be rightfully proud. Unity is no Eastern religion or occult practice; it is a direct descendent of a long history of Christian mysticism. As Charles Fillmore wrote: *Unity is a link in the great educational movement inaugurated by Jesus Christ. . . . The truth that we teach is not new, neither do we claim special revelations or discovery of new religious principles. Our purpose is to help and teach mankind to use and prove the eternal Truth taught by the Master.*[165]

What better news could we hear than news of others throughout the ages and into the present being heir to the same mission? What better vision of tomorrow could there be than the movement of all consciousness toward the Omega Point, toward Christ consciousness? The time is fast approaching when more and more people will realize the Truth taught by great Christian thinkers down through the ages: the future is not a bleak rush toward oblivion, but a grand reconvening of all sentient beings, unity in all things.

Afterword

Now we have a beginning. There is much work yet to be done before mystical/metaphysical Christianity speaks the language of modern theology. The benefits to be gained in such a breakthrough will bless Truth churches, which have much to learn about their heritage in Western mystical theology, and the mainline churches of today, which hunger for spiritual renewal but shy away from the fundamentalist born-again movement because it fails to meet their needs for an inclusive religious faith.

Unity is in a unique position to offer its

services as a bridge builder. Our background studies clearly show that practical spirituality stands in the mainstream of the mystical Christian heritage when it affirms the divinity in every human being. Unity could offer its understandings to vast multitudes who yearn for a faith that works in the marketplace as well as on Sundays. But to bridge the gap between our *weltanschauung* and the thought-world of modern Protestant theology, we must first understand what we share with mystics of yesterday and today. Orthodoxy needs our vitality and insights; we need a sense of the ancient church as our homeland and heritage.

This study has explored how deep our roots run. It has attempted to find common ground with some of the great thinkers of Christian history. Beyond historical analysis, it has also suggested that we stand at the cutting edge of the theology of tomorrow. The implication of such a vantage point is clear: those with special gifts have special responsibilities to share the great mystical insights of practical Christianity with our brothers and sisters in the ancient faith. Therefore, we must speak the language of modern theology. This is the driving force behind these surveys in mystical theology through the study of mystical theologians.

I see a Christian faith emerging in the twenty-first century that is conscious of its past and active in the world today. I see groups and churches dedicated to affirmative prayer and meditation springing up in all the denominations of Christianity's great family of faiths. I see a new surge in the eternal, upward struggle toward Christ consciousness, prompted by the longing of people for a taste of God's presence in their increasingly complex, computer-enhanced lives. I see world spiritual consciousness, replacing ethnocentric race consciousness, when people begin to see themselves as citizens of one world/nation and begin to feel that their first loyalties are and ought to be toward the divine Spirit within people everywhere. I see freedom spreading its blessings of spiritual liberty across the face of our world. I see one people, the human race, worshiping one Power and one Presence, God, the good omnipotent.

And I see Unity smiling as it leads the movement toward oneness, knowing where it came from, knowing where it is, and excited about where it is going.

Dreams of utopia? Hardly. There will be no

utopia until all sentient beings are fully aware of their oneness with God, and frankly that may take quite some time. But if the driving, compelling, overpowering passion of the human family becomes the upward quest for political, social, and spiritual unity in the freedom that God has intended for all of us, perhaps this world will become a little more like an outpost of the kingdom of heaven. I dream of the day when all humanity chants the great prayer of James Dillet Freeman as a testimony to its hopes for oneness:

The light of God surrounds us;
The love of God enfolds us;
The power of God protects us;
The presence of God watches over us.
Wherever we are, God is!

When Unity becomes fully aware of the role it has to play in the spiritual future of humanity, that day might come sooner than we think.

Footnotes

Chapter 1

[1]Samuel Sandmel, *Philo of Alexandria* (New York: Oxford University Press, 1979), pp. 6-7.

[2]Paul Johnson, *A History of Christianity* (New York: Atheneum, 1980), p. 48.

[3]David Winston, *Philo of Alexandria* (New York: Paulist Press, 1981), p. 2.

[4]*Metaphysical Bible Dictionary* (Kansas City, MO: Unity Books, 1942), p. 461.

[5]Charles Fillmore, *The Revealing Word* (Unity Village, MO: Unity Books, 1979), p. 136.

[6]Dagobert D. Runes, (ed.), *Treasury of World Philosophy* (Patterson, NJ: Littlefield, Adams & Co., 1959), p. 1256.

[7]*Ibid.*, p. 1257.

[8]Winston, p. 6.

[9]Sandmel, p. 28.

[10]*Ibid.*

[11]*Metaphysical Bible Dictionary*, p. 8.

[12]Charles Fillmore, *Atom-Smashing Power of Mind* (Unity Village, MO: Unity Books, 1949), p. 80.

[13]Sandmel, pp. 84, 88, 100.

[14]*Ibid.*, p. 46.

[15]*Ibid.*

[16]*Ibid.*

[17]The Bible. Revised Standard Version.

Chapter 2

18Jonas C. Greenfield, "The History of Israel, Part II," *The Interpreter's One Volume Commentary on the Bible*, ed. Charles M. Laymon (Nashville, TN: Abingdon, 1971), pp. 1030-1.

19The Bible. Revised Standard Version.

20*Ibid.*

21Tertullian, *Apologeticus adversus Gentes pro Christianis*, MSL, I:525.

22Han Urs Von Balthasar, Preface to *Origen*, ed. Rowan A. Greer, (New York: Paulist Press, 1979), p. xii.

23Johnson, p. 58.

24*Ibid.*

25Rowan A. Greer, (ed.), *Origen* (New York: Paulist Press, 1979), p. 2

26Arthur Cushman McGiffert, *A History of Christian Thought*, Vol. I (New York: Charles Scribner's Sons, 1932), p. 229.

27*Ibid.*, pp. 225-226.

28Greer, pp. 8-9.

29George W. Anderson, "The History of Biblical Interpretation," *The Interpreter's One Volume Commentary on the Bible*, ed. Charles M. Laymon (Nashville, TN: Abingdon, 1971), p. 973.

30*Ibid.*

31Origen, "On First Principles," *Origen*, ed. Rowan A. Greer, (New York: Paulist Press, 1979), p. 196.

32Origen, *On First Principles*, trans. G. W. Butterworth (New York: Harper Torchbooks, 1966), p. 327.

Chapter 3

[33]William Butler Yeats, Untitled Poem, *Origen,* ed. Rowan A. Greer (New York: Paulist Press, 1979), pp. 1-2.

[34]Johnson, p. 86.

[35]*Ibid.,* p. 112.

[36]*Ibid.,* p. 122.

[37]Arthur Cushman McGiffert, *A History of Christian Thought,* Vol. II (New York: Charles Scribner's Sons, 1933), p. 128.

[38]Paul Tillich, *A History of Christian Thought* (New York: Simon & Schuster, 1968), p. 123.

[39]The Bible. Revised Standard Version.

[40]Johnson, p. 229.

[41]McGiffert, pp. 125-126.

[42]Johnson, p. 123.

[43]*Ibid.,* p. 120.

[44]Robert Payne, *The Horizon Book of Ancient Rome* (New York: American Heritage, 1966), p. 366.

[45]*Ibid.*

[46]Joseph Cullen Ayer, Jr., *A Source Book for Ancient Church History* (New York: Charles Scribner's Sons, 1913), p. 373.

[47]*Ibid.,* pp. 373-374.

[48]*Ibid.*

Chapter 4

49Tillich, p. 90.

50M. R. James, *The Apocryphal New Testament* (London: Oxford University Press, 1966), pp. vi-x.

51The Bible. Revised Standard Version.

52Tillich, p. 90.

53Arthur Cushman McGiffert, *A History of Christian Thought,* Vol. I (New York: Charles Scribner's Sons, 1960), p. 293.

54*Ibid.*

55Charles Fillmore, *Talks on Truth* (Unity Village, MO: Unity Books, 1934), p. 60.

56C. E. Rolt (trans.) *Dionysius the Areopagite* (New York: The Macmillan Co., 1951), p. 100.

57*Ibid.,* p. 101.

58*Ibid.,* pp. 111-112.

59*Ibid.,* p. 114.

60*Ibid.,* pp. 120-121.

61McGiffert, pp. 304-305.

62*Ibid.*

63H. Emilie Cady, *Lessons in Truth* (Unity Village, MO: Unity Books), pp. 34, 35.

Chapter 5

64Johnson, p. 157.

65*Ibid.*

66Will Durant, *The Story of Civilization,* Vol. IV, *The Age of Faith* (New York: Simon & Schuster, 1950), p. 477.

67*Ibid.*

68McGiffert, p. 173.

69*Ibid.*
70McGiffert, p. 170.
71Durant, p. 477.
72*Ibid.*
73McGiffert, p. 169.

Chapter 6

74Walter Holden Capps and Wendy M. Wright, (eds.), *Silent Fire* (San Francisco: Harper Forum Books, 1978), pp. 112, 114.
75*Ibid.,* p. 115.
76Tillich, p. 201.
77Arthur Cushman McGiffert, *A History of Christian Thought,* Vol. II (New York: Charles Scribner's Sons, 1933), p. 260.
78*Ibid.*
79*Ibid.*
80For a more comprehensive treatment of Aquinas's struggles with the Platonic-Aristotelian synthesis, see the chapter on Thomas Aquinas in *A History of Christian Thought,* Vol. II, by McGiffert.
81Capps & Wright, p. 111.
82McGiffert, pp. 360-361.
83*Ibid.,* p. 362.
84*Ibid.*
85Edmund Colledge and Bernard McGinn (trans.), *Meister Eckhart, Classics of Western Spirituality* (New York: Paulist Press, 1981), p. 207.
86McGiffert, p. 371.
87*Ibid.,* p. 365.
88*Ibid.,* pp. 362-363.

Chapter 7

89Howard H. Brinton, The Religion of George Fox (Lebanon, PA: Pendle Hill, 1968), p. 11.

90Will Durant, *The Story of Civilization,* Vol. VI: *The Reformation* (New York: Simon & Schuster, 1957), p. 532.

91*Ibid.*

92Edith Simon, *The Great Age of Man: The Reformation* (Alexandria, VA: Time-Life Books, Inc., 1966), p. 82.

93Henry Van Etten, *George Fox and the Quakers,* trans. E. Kelvin Osborn (New York: Harper Torchbooks, 1959), p. 9.

94William Penn, "The Testimony of William Penn Concerning That Faithful Servant, George Fox," *The Journal of George Fox,* ed. Rufas M. Jones (New York: Capricorn Books, 1963), p. 50.

95Rufas M. Jones (ed.), *The Journal of George Fox,* p. 70.

96*Ibid.,* p. 530.

97*Ibid.,* p. 73.

98D. Elton Trueblood, *The People Called Quakers* (New York: Harper & Row, 1966), p. 22.

99Jones, p. 150.

100Martin E. Marty, *A Short History of Christianity* (Cleveland, Ohio: World Publishing Co., 1966), p. 265.

101Jones, pp. 101-102, 105.

102*Ibid.*

[103]Van Etten, p. 86.
[104]Jones, p. 427.
[105]*Ibid.*, p. 82.
[106]Brinton, p. 10.

Chapter 8

[107]Charles Fillmore, *The Twelve Powers of Man* (Unity Village, MO: Unity Books), p. 83.
[108]Daniel Defoe, *Robinson Crusoe* (Boston: Houghton Mifflin Co., 1937) pp. 314-315.
[109]John Macquarrie, *Twentieth-Century Religious Thought* (London: SCM Press, Ltd., 1971), p. 24.
[110]Cady, p. 44.
[111]Charles Fillmore, *The Revealing Word* (Unity Village, MO: Unity Books, 1979), p. 64.
[112]Macquarrie, p. 24.
[113]Charles Fillmore, *Mysteries of Genesis* (Unity Village, MO: Unity Books), p. 57.
[114]Maurice Nicoll, *Psychological Commentaries on the Teaching of G. I. Gurdjieff and P. D. Ouspensky,* Vol. I (London: Stuart & Watkins, 1970), p. 108.
[115]*Ibid.*, p. 109.
[116]Georg Wilhelm Friedrich Hegel, "The Philosophy of History," *Great Books of the Western World,* Vol. 46, *Hegel,* Robert Maynard Hutchins, editor-in-chief (Chicago: University of Chicago, 1952), p. 1596.

Chapter 9

117Ralph Waldo Emerson, "The Divinity School Address," *Three Prophets of Religious Liberalism,* Conrad Wright, (ed.) (Boston: Beacon Press, 1961), pp. 107-108.

118Theodore Parker, "The Transient and Permanent in Christianity," *Three Prophets of Religious Liberalism,* pp. 140-141.

119George N. Marshall, *Challenge of a Liberal Faith* (New Canaan, CT: 1980), pp. 106-107.

120Ralph Waldo Emerson, "Threnody," *Selected Prose and Poetry,* Reginald L. Cook, (ed.) (New York: Holt, Rinehart & Winston, 1969), p. 447.

121Earl Morse Wilbur, *Our Unitarian Heritage* (Boston, Beacon Press, 1963), p. 434.

122Emerson, *Three Prophets of Religious Liberalism,* pp. 96-97.

123*Ibid.,* p. 97.

124*Ibid.*

125*Ibid.*

126Emerson, p. 99.

127John Weiss, *Life and Correspondence of Theodore Parker* (New York: Arno Press, 1969), p.119.

128Wilbur, p. 434.

129Cady, pp. 72-73.

130Emerson packet, unsigned, "Anecdotes" sheet (Boston: Emerson Commemorative Committee, 1982), side one.

131Wilbur, p. 437.

[132]Theodore Parker, *Three Prophets of Religious Liberalism,* p. 118.

[133]Weiss, p. 72.

[134]Weiss, p. 83.

Chapter 10

[135]Nona Brooks, *Divine Science* (Denver, CO: Divine Science Federation, 1957), pp. 11-12.

[136]Joseph Cullen, *A Source Book for Ancient Church History* (New York: Scribner's, 1913), p. 52.

[137]Dr. D. Patterson, Letter to P. P. Quimby, *The Quimby Manuscripts,* Horatio Dresser, (ed.) (Secausus, NJ: The Citadel Press, 1980), pp. 152-153.

[138]Mary Baker Eddy, *Science and Health* (Boston: First Church of Christ, Scientist, 1971), p. 1.

[139]Charles S. Braden, *Spirits in Rebellion* (Dallas, TX: Southern Methodist University Press, 1980), p. 235.

[140]Eddy, p. 472.

[141]Braden, p. 143.

[142]*Ibid.,* p. 140.

[143]*Ibid.,* p. 141.

[144]Emma Curtis Hopkins, *Scientific Christian Mental Practice* (Marina del Rey, CA: DeVorss, undated), p. 36.

[145]*Ibid.,* p. 37.

[146]Hazel Deane, *Powerful is the Light* (Denver, CO: Divine Science Federation, 1945), p. 44.

[147]*Ibid.,* p. 88.

Chapter 11

[148]Paul Tillich, *Systematic Theology Volume One* (Chicago: University of Chicago, 1951), p. 16.

[149]*Ibid.*, p. 235.

[150]Cady, p. 22.

[151]Tillich, p. 239.

[152]*Ibid.*, p. 244.

[153]T. A. Kantonen, *Christian Faith Today: Studies in Contemporary Theology* (Lima, Ohio: C.S.S. Publishing Co., 1974), p. 42.

[154]John A. T. Robinson, *Honest to God* (Philadelphia: Westminster Press, 1963).

Chapter 12

[155]The Bible. Revised Standard Version.

[156]Kantonen, p. 80.

[157]*Ibid.*, p. 85.

[158]*Ibid.*, pp. 91-92.

[159]Marcus Bach, *The Unity Way* (Unity Village, MO: Unity Books, 1982), pp. 357-358.

[160]*Ibid.*, pp. 358-359.

[161]Kantonen, p. 87.

[162]*Ibid.*, p. 85.

[163]*Ibid.*, p. 89.

[164]Teilhard de Chardin, "Hymn of the Universe," *Silent Fire*, Walter Holden Capps and Wendy M. Wright, (eds.) (New York: Harper Forum Books, 1978), p. 237.

[165]Charles Fillmore, *Dynamics for Living* (Unity Village, MO: Unity Books, 1967), p. 2.

About the Author

Thomas Shepherd is a long-time Unity student and teacher. He has served as principal speaker in several Unity centers, where he has also taught classes. He is an ordained minister with the Unitarian-Universalist Association and the Congregational Christian Church. His "main ambition" is to become a Unity minister "in a successful, prosperous Unity center."

A Vietnam War veteran, he was awarded the Air Medal, the Purple Heart, the Vietnamese Cross of Gallantry, and twice the Distinguished Flying Cross. He has also served as an Army Chaplain in West Germany.

Shepherd graduated cum laude with a BS in Education in Social Studies from the University of Idaho, and he graduated magna cum laude with a M.Div. from the Lancaster theological Seminary in Lancaster, Pennsylvania. He has written several articles for professional journals and for UNITY Magazine.

He is married to the former Carol Jean Loos, who has also taught at Unity centers and was a sponsor of the Denver, Colorado Youth of Unity for seven years.

Printed U.S.A.

170-F-8135-10M-2-86